BACK *to the* LOCAL

'Wonderful . . . a detailed study of life in London pubs.'
Islington Tribune

'Probably the most delightful and evocative book ever produced
on the English pub.' *Slightly Foxed*

'In *Back to the Local*, Maurice Gorham and Edward Ardizzone
cast an affectionate glance over the private lives of public houses.
One day all pubs will be like this.'
**Andy Miller, author of *The Year of Reading Dangerously*,
co-host of Backlisted podcast**

'This little gem of a book first published just after the Second
World War shows that the London pub has always been under
threat from brewers, bureaucrats, developers, temperance
campaigners, rationalisers and philistines of all stripes. The author
Maurice Gorham paints a picture that is in some ways completely
familiar, of the disappearance of charismatic backstreet locals, and
in other ways totally alien, as beer was still being rationed when
he was researching it. Sadly a lot of the pubs he writes about have
gone the way of the great London brewers like Truman, Hanbury
& Buxton which must have seemed so mighty in the 1940s,
but some have survived and we should treasure them and, most
importantly, visit them. A good pub has to be a living institution,
not a museum or a tourist destination.'
**Henry Jeffreys, author of *Empire of Booze*
and *Vines in a Cold Climate***

'It vividly brings to life a lost world of haughty barmaids,
snack bars and after hours loitering, recorded with wit,
affection and a killer ⸺ ⸺ ⸺ ⸺ ⸺'
John Grindrod, author of *Icon*⸺
Landmark Buildings of C ⸺

T0182617

The Warwick Castle

BACK *to the* LOCAL

by
MAURICE GORHAM

Illustrations by
EDWARD ARDIZZONE

faber

This edition first published in 2024
by Faber & Faber Ltd
The Bindery, 51 Hatton Garden
London ECIN 8HN

First published in 1949 by Cassell & Co, Ltd

Printed by TJ Books Limited, Padstow, Cornwall

A CIP record for this book
is available from the British Library

ISBN 978-0-571-38698-7

MIX
Paper from
responsible sources
FSC® C013056

Printed and bound in the UK on FSC® certified paper in line with our continuing
commitment to ethical business practices, sustainability and the environment.
For further information see faber.co.uk/environmental-policy

2 4 6 8 10 9 7 5 3 1

PREFACE

'**D**O YOU FANCY A PINT?' For those of us of a bibulous bent, that is perhaps the most welcome question in the English language. Who can resist a cheery invitation to enjoy a large cold glass in a small warm snug, or maybe a rollicking round in a busy and convivial local? It is the eternal lure of the perfect pub; good beer and splendid company in the comely comfort of a charismatic and well-kept house. And for those of a bibliophile bent, this lovely little book is the literary equivalent. I defy you to read this intoxicating tome and not fancy a pint or two every page.

Back to the Local was written by Maurice (I feel like we are now on first name terms) back in 1949, when the licensed trade was slowly returning to something like normality after the tumult of bombings, closures and beer shortages of the war-time period. London lost a number of great old taverns to the Luftwaffe and this book is a lovingly compiled inventory of the city's survivors by a man who certainly knows his pickled onions.

It is essentially a languorous crawl around the remaining public houses and hostelries of a London town recovering from the severe bashing it received during the Blitz. You can almost taste the relief at having lived to sup another day, and the delight in the knowledge, that despite the carnage, so many historic old public houses were still standing.

Written in the conversational but gently lyrical style of the time – a little like Betjemen on boozers – it is effortlessly, charmingly old-fashioned (and I don't mean the cocktail, this is strictly a beer book). It feels like a chat with a knowledgeable and worldly chap who you've just met in the saloon bar of a particularly alluring backstreet hostelry. A chap who somehow knows every pub in town.

Clearly a lifetime's labour of love, *Back to the Local* is full of great anecdotes and sage opinions. Some of it is, of course, dated: there are not too many jug-and-bottle bars around today; itinerant penny-whistle players are not as prominent as they once were; and you can no longer get a pint of stout for a shilling; but the allure of the pub is timeless and his observations priceless.

Maurice is a wonderfully knowledgeable guide but also a pointed critic. He is not fond of what he calls 'the flash', the bright and brash young things who frequent the modern-style pubs he detests and play darts with undue gusto. Rather, he favours cheery landlords, mahogany bars, dark beers, good manners, communality and decency, yet gently laments the fact that you rarely see a decent punch-up in a London pub anymore.

As well as the wise and witty words, there are also the fantastic, impressionistic illustrations. The brilliant Edward Ardizonne executes his fluid pen and ink drawings in an almost Ealing-Comedy black and white, redolent of scenes in *Passport to Pimlico* or *The Lavender Hill Mob*. This series of elegantly wonky sketches of pub interiors and the punters in them, somehow captures the woozy atmosphere of life inside the confines of the unique institution which is the British public house.

From the very first pub on the very first page, *Back to the Local* engenders the slightly sozzled atmosphere of that second drink, when the air has started to become warm and fuzzy and all is well with your world. This book is like a great pub itself; easy to enter, but tough to leave, as you savour every word and enjoy every last drop of the intense flavours of the time.

For this is a portrait of a city told through its lowly ale houses and posh parlours, its ancient and crooked taverns and its swanky gin palaces. London is a city of constant change, a shape-shifting metropolis, which is perpetually reinventing itself, yet which somehow stays the same. And the same is true of its pubs. What is most remarkable and loveable about *Back to the Local* is just how much of it still applies today.

There were roughly four thousand pubs in London in 1949, and there are just a couple of hundred shy of that today (plus a multitude of wine and cocktail bars, which barely existed back then). And despite being over eighty years old, you could still use this book as a back-pocket guide to your well-lubricated inner-city perambulations, because the vast majority of the famous old houses he loved so much and described so well are still with us: The Cheshire Cheese, the Angel and the Prospect of Whitby, the Dover Castle, the French House (formerly the York Minster) and the Town of Ramsgate, The Friend at Hand, the Coal

Hole and the Cittie of Yorke . . . hundreds of timelessly terrific pubs with great stories to tell. Drink in one of those now and you can still experience the architecture and atmosphere Maurice Gorham relished.

There are, of course, differences: the strict social divisions of public and saloon bar have all but gone; food is much more important – the boom in gastropubs was still half a century away when Maurice was tucking into the occasional pork pie; and pints of 'mild' have largely disappeared. Today you can get decent wine in almost every London boozer (back then it was just port and sherry for the ladies), while lager has replaced ale as the most popular drink.

But the very fact that London pubs are still just as popular, just as much part of the fabric of the city, is testament to their durability. They survived the Blitz, the town planners and even a recent pandemic, and have made it through to today intact. And so, thankfully, has this splendid little edition. Do I fancy a pint? I'll meet you in my local.

ROBERT ELMS, 2024

FOREWORD

SHORTLY before the war Ted Ardizzone and I worked together on a book about London pubs, which we called 'The Local'. By the time it appeared the war had begun, and the book's career ended when unsold copies, sheets, and plates of the drawings went up together in the burning of Cassells' premises in Belle Sauvage Yard.

Before that consummation overtook it, the book had been well enough received to make us feel it would be worth while to tackle the subject again, and we were the more easily persuaded because there is no subject that we both enjoy tackling more.

Of course things have changed since 1939: pubs, pub-goers, drinking habits, even ourselves. So although this book follows the same scheme as 'The Local' it is a different book. Ardizzone has re-drawn the same subjects, though not quite in the same way, and added some more; I have rewritten and added to the text, to take account of things as they are now. By courtesy of Messrs. Cassell some of the same material is included, notably the Glossary, but this of course has had to be heavily revised. An index of pubs has been added. On my side some omissions have been rectified and one or two glaring errors, which I am glad to say nobody appears to have noticed except myself.

There may still of course be errors and omissions, for which I apologise in advance. If there are not more that is due to the help I have had from many pub-goers and landlords to whom I have talked, and in particular to Ralph Hill, Kelly Bartels, and Colonel R. M. Furber, of SHAEF and the U.S. Treasury, who gave me the facts about American as compared with British measures, on which I went very wrong in *The Local*. None of them of course necessarily shares all my views.

Things are still changing too, and it is hard to keep up to date. The beer shortage that hung over London when I was writing most of this book has passed away, but who knows whether the next hot weather may not bring it again? The Licensing Bill has come to make the very mention of pubs more than ever controversial, and I had better say here that this book is not written to advance the views of any of the organised interests—brewers, planners, reformers, or anybody else. So far as it represents anybody it represents the least organised of all the interests—the people who go to their local to have a drink. But Ardizzone and I do not even claim to be typical pub-goers: merely enthusiastic pub-goers, who use the London pubs habitually and hope to go on using them for a long time.

We both hope that this book will appeal to people who still enjoy going to a pub, and especially to those who have come back to their local and found that in spite of all the changes it still has a part to play in their lives. The changes are not all for the worse; the local still offers some things that you can't get elsewhere; and we trust that we ourselves have not altogether lost the innocent enthusiasms of 1939.

London 1948-9

CONTENTS

INTRODUCTORY

SINCE the war ended a lot of people have been trying to revive the habits they most enjoyed before 1939, and one of the most widespread of these habits is visiting the local. The pleasure that this habit affords is not perhaps lofty but it is very profound, and as dearly prized by Londoners who have a pub in every street as by country-dwellers who may have only one within miles. During the war, certainly, it was one of the habits they missed most. Whether they were parching in the desert, evacuated with their jobs to unfamiliar seaside towns or country villages or inland spas, or merely working night shift, many of them were thinking and talking mainly about the time when they would again be able to drop into the old friendly local and have a pint or two among their friends.

Some of them came back to find their local gone, but they were the unlucky ones; like most things, the pubs survived the war better than seemed likely at one time. All of them found changes. The local might not open at all on Sunday, or it might close early on Saturday night. The fatal words 'Finished serving' rang even more bleakly on the ear than the old familiar cry of 'Time'.

But London still has most of its 4,000 pubs, and they still number amongst them pubs of every kind. Old, sham-old, and comparatively new; prosperous and neglected, smart and shabby; pubs standing forlornly in the midst of bomb-damage, with their top storey missing and one bar gone, and pubs lurking safely under the great piles of modern office blocks. There are pubs that were the pride of the rebuilders in 1939, and pubs that were scheduled for demolition and have been saved by the war; pubs that have taken their place among the sights of London and pubs that are unknown two streets away.

Nobody can profess to know all the pubs of London, and Ardizzone and I certainly make no such claim. We cannot even feel confident that we know enough about pubs to be able to generalise; among the few thousand that we have not come across, there may be enough exceptions to change all the rules.

But all the pubs I have ever used have one thing in common. Each one is somebody's local. Each one has its regular customers who use it, for some reason, in preference to other pubs. It may be the nearest to where they live or work, but it may not. One of the saddest things about the beer shortage has been its unsettling effect on the regulars who, after walking past the Pineapple on their way to the Phoenix, find the Phoenix closed and have to walk back to the Pineapple again. But they still make the hopeful journey, and even if you have never spoken to them or they to you, you look at each other sympathetically when you finally stand side by side in the alien bar.

They all have their regulars. Even the sightseers' pubs; there is no greater show-place in London than the Cheshire Cheese off Fleet Street, but its bar is used regularly by journalists, advertising men, photographers—all sorts of local workers who would never think of ordering the famous pudding, nor derive any satisfaction from sitting in Doctor Johnson's seat. There are pubs that have a lower proportion of regulars than the average, but even the biggest pubs on circuses— the sort that bus-stops are named after—and the busiest station bars seem to have customers who ask for 'the usual' and call the barmaids by their first names.

Of course, there is no reason why one person should not have more than one local. In the more favoured parts of London you may have two or three near your home and another two or three near the place where you work, apart from any that happen to be conveniently situated, for instance at bus-stops and stations, between the two. How many pubs you use regularly depends upon your own taste and fancy and the extent to which you expect different things from pubs at different times. If you want to become an intimate of the house it is of course best to use as few houses as possible so as to use those few more, but if your ambition is merely to be nodded to when you come in, and sometimes to be served before you give an order, that degree of familiarity can be attained in a score of houses without any danger of drinking yourself to death. Even in these days, when barmaids and managers seem to be always on the move, the people who work in pubs are fairly observant and know their customers better than you would think. You find the proof of this when they move. A landlord who has never shown any sign of recognition in his old house will no sooner see you enter his new house than he hails you as an old friend, and it can be quite embarrassing to go into an unfamiliar pub and be greeted by a half-remembered barmaid with 'Well, fancy that now. Who told you I'd come here?'

Other People's Locals

This possible plurality of locals is the only excuse for this book. Anybody who really likes pubs can have quite a lot of locals of his own; he will enjoy visiting his friends in *their* locals; and he will find that to sample other people's locals is one way of learning how the other half lives.

Your own local can be a club, a refuge, a home from home. But an enquiring spirit will feel sooner or later the stirrings of desire for discovery. Other pubs tempt you; you go home a different way, or get off the bus at a different place, to try the pub that you have always noticed and never visited; you let your walks lead you to pubs that you have passed when you were in a hurry or when they were closed; you begin to be curious about the pubs of the East End or the West End, as the case may be; you wonder whether the pubs of Chelsea or Chiswick, Hampstead or Highgate, are all that they are cracked up to be; you hear that a rare brew is on sale at some out-of-the-way London pub and you decide to go and find it. You make many discoveries and you draw many blanks. If the proportion of discoveries is high enough you reach the condition when you collect pubs hopefully, as a gourmet collects restaurants, and a pub you have not sampled becomes a challenge to go in.

This, of course, is a long job, if you are not to neglect your own locals whilst you explore. And it is an endless job. As you add to your list of pubs visited, you leave behind you an ever-increasing list of pubs to be visited again. There are those you found good enough to visit for pleasure, and those you found bad enough to make you wonder whether you were wrong the first time.

And any pub may have changed since you were there last. The changes are not so drastic now as they were before the war, when the brewers were busy pulling down houses in all directions under the twin slogans of Rebuilding and Redundancy; nor as they were during the bombing, when one had to have second and third strings for appointments made a day ahead ('I'll meet you at Ward's Irish House

3

in Piccadilly Circus; or if that's gone, at the Standard across the way; and failing that, at the Punch House behind the Haymarket'); nor even as they were towards the end of the war, when bombed houses that one had written off would suddenly reopen and bring a new interest to life. But pubs still sometimes change brewers, let alone staff. You may be passing a pub that you have not been to for some months and think 'I wonder if they've still got that nice barmaid', or 'that friendly landlord', or even 'that hideous old harridan who was so rude when I asked for a box of matches', and in you go again.

The rewards of exploration are high. Pubs vary so prodigiously and so unexpectedly. You find them in all sorts of places, and you find all sorts of people in them. Neither neighbourhood nor exterior is any guide to what is within. A house with a long imposing façade may turn out to be only a few feet deep; a house with a modest entrance and a narrow frontage may stretch back to the next street, as do some of the pubs in Fleet Street and the Strand. Only the other day I was taken to a little country-like pub with an entrance up some steps in a mews, and the friend whose local it was laughed cruelly at my disillusionment when he led me through to the Saloon and we found ourselves among the white-collared habitués of the Harrington Hotel in Gloucester Road.

You can still find plebeian houses in expensive neighbourhoods, though you will find fewer and fewer of them, for the brewers have discovered them too and are doing all they can to make their revenues more consistent with their ground rents; and you can find the neatest and snuggest of houses in the dingiest streets (who, for instance, could wish for a trimmer place to lunch than the Saloon Bar of the White Horse in Poplar High Street, just before it runs into Pennyfields; and where could you find a brighter bar than at the Steam Packet amongst the coal-tips and the bomb damage in Nine Elms Lane?). Even the modernisation may be only skin-deep; it is true that sometimes an ancient exterior conceals a bar all light oak and linoleum, but many a glazed-tile front leads into an unimpaired Victorian bar.

As for the people, in London pubs you see Londoners, and as Dr. Johnson might have put it, the man who is tired of Londoners is tired of mankind. But if you want specialisation you can always find the specialised pubs. Sometimes they can be deduced from their surroundings but more often not. You would expect, for instance, to find a

Continental atmosphere in the Swiss Hotel in Old Compton Street, but why should the Helvetia further up the road be quite normally English, whilst the York Minster in Dean Street confronts you with a wall-full of photographs of French boxers and cyclists, and French spoken freely on both sides of the bar? (The answer here, of course, is the Berlemont family; M. Victor's superb moustaches long reigned unique in the victualling trade, but now there is a landlord at the Grenadier in Old Barrack Yard who is making a bold bid for the title, and he has youth on his side). You would expect to find the BBC dominant in the pubs around Portland Place, but unless you know all its multifarious addresses you may be surprised to find it equally conspicious in such houses as the Rose of Normandy in Marylebone High Street and the Coach and Horses in Bruton Street. There are many pubs around Archer Street, but the Lyric Tavern is the one where everybody who comes into the Saloon Bar seems to be in the dance-music business. If I want to overhear the couriers meeting and exchanging their cosmopolitan Cockney, the place I try first, of all the pubs around Victoria, is the Grosvenor Basin in Wilton Road.

There are the stage-door pubs, like the Grapes behind the Palladium, where the clientèle varies with the bill of the week, and the Victoria Stores behind the Victoria Palace, where you can see the chorus-boys, all made up for the second house, struggling to the bar through the press of broad-backed draymen from Watney's brewery at the end of the road. The Nag's Head in Floral Street used to have the custom of Jackson, the celebrated stage-door keeper of Covent Garden, as well as *Daily Herald* men from Long Acre, detectives from Bow Street, and fruit salesmen from the market; the George in Mortimer Street is a traditional haunt of musicians and enjoys also the patronage of the used-car salesmen, the Rag Trade (or wholesale dress business), and of course the BBC. The busmen frequent the Lord Burleigh in Vauxhall Bridge Road; the private-hire drivers meet in the mews pubs near their garages but I don't know why I always seem to meet them at the Devonshire Arms in Pimlico as well; there is a pub I know where the deaf-and-dumb congregate, and you suddenly become aware of a pool of silence in the chatter of the bar. There used to be a pub not far from Seven Dials where you would find car thieves who stopped talking when you went in, but long ago they closed it down.

You expect to find specialised clientèles in the pubs of Wardour Street, Billingsgate, Fleet Street, and other neighbourhoods which are the centres of trades. If you know the neighbourhood or the trade well enough you probably learn that each has its subdivisions, and it may, for all I know, be as rare for a sports-writer to go into the Welsh Harp in Temple Lane as for a stereotyper to go into the Red Lion in Poppin's Court. The highly specialised pubs are comparatively rare, though you may stumble on one of them at any time. But you can always count on differences of atmosphere, architecture, personnel, and even drinks—for different houses can serve very different versions of the same brew.

Extensive and Peculiar

The real value of knowing your pubs was excellently displayed by Mr. Weller when Mr. Pickwick, feeling rather ruffled after his interview with Dodson and Fogg, expressed a desire for a glass of brandy and water warm and asked Sam where he could have it. Mr. Weller's knowledge of London was extensive and peculiar. He replied, without the slightest consideration:

> 'Second court on the right hand side—last house but vun on the same side the vay—take the box as stands in the first fire-place, 'cos there an't no leg in the middle o' the table, wich all the others has, and it's wery inconwenient.'

Sam had had exceptional advantages in the way of education, as his father remarked on that very occasion, and he was not handicapped by closing-times, beer shortages, and all the other tribulations that beset the pub-user of today. But these limitations only make the knowledge more important, and it is uncommonly useful to have a local wherever you happen to be, especially if you can feel sure that it really is the best pub in the neighbourhood and not merely the best that you know.

Some of the nicest pubs in London are well hidden from the casual view. One of the chief interests of exploratory walks is in finding them and noting them for future use—for nobody can tell when and where he will meet his Dodson and Fogg.

Sometimes, indeed, these by-street pubs are indispensable, when the main streets have none. Few of London's main thoroughfares are so barren; Whitehall, Sloane Street, Curzon Street, Wigmore Street (to name a few of the less likely ones) all have their pubs. Park Lane has its pub, but if you have followed the bus route from Marble Arch to the fountain and go on following it down Hamilton Place you will miss the Rose and Crown that nestles shyly in the narrow end of the true Park Lane, and you may well arrive at Victoria thirsty. Yet from Mount Street down, almost any detour would have brought you to a pub—perhaps the Audley Hotel in Mount Street, the Punch Bowl in Farm Street, the Red Lion in Waverton Street, the new Shepherds, or the original Mayfair Hotel.

Going on towards Victoria you come to another arid patch. Grosvenor Place has not a single pub until you get to the corner by the station. But just parallel to it there is a perfect avenue of pubs.

The bar of the Alexandra has demolition hanging over its head as I write, but in the mews behind Wilton Crescent lurks the Grenadier, and between Halkin Street and Wilton Street you will find the Coachmakers' Arms, the Horse and Groom, the Stanhope, and the Nottingham Castle, all small, local, pleasant, giving choice of several different brews. And these are only a remnant in what was once a really well-served neighbourhood. The Talbot in Little Chester Street was bombed, and where you used to be able to go down the last mews to the back door of the Feathers, emerge in the Public Bar (at the risk of getting a dart in your eye as you opened the door) and so into Hobart Place, you now encounter the grim bulk of Hobart House. The Feathers must have been one of the last pubs to be slaughtered before the war.

It is the same with Bond Street, Regent Street, Pall Mall; they may have no pubs of their own, but keep a keen eye open for the side turnings, the courts and the alleys, and you will never have far to go. The most desperate neighbourhoods are outside central London, in the newer quarters where streets are longer and whole neighbourhoods were planned in an unfriendly age. You can have anxious moments as closing-time draws near and finds you marooned halfway down Castelnau or the Cromwell Road.

Even in some of the older parts you may have to think quickly. Pimlico, with all its handsome vistas, is well supplied with pubs, but it has had more than its share of war losses and you may strike a bad patch around where the Monster used to be; the White Ferry House is the last survivor of four, and woe betide you if it is closed. Most of the older squares have mews and back-streets that never fail, but I have had a moment of panic in Russell Square until I realised that the people who work in the big hotels cannot possibly drink in them, and found the well-named Friend at Hand lurking behind. The City of London itself, old as it is, has been rebuilt with such emphasis on big business and so little on ordinary life that the stranger may find himself hard set to spy a sign more hospitable than the sign of an insurance company, and there again I have been most grateful for the unexpected discovery of such an oasis as the Three Crowns in Old Jewry, with its discreet Saloon entrance in Dove Court.

There is a special category of useful knowledge relating to pubs of refuge and escape; the pubs that lie near other places where you have to go and can't get draught beer. In my time I have suffered much from business lunches and official dinners where there is every sort of luxury except a couple of pints. If you are prudent you will nip into a pub beforehand, but after an hour or two of food, short drinks, and possibly speeches, your thoughts begin to turn to pubs again, and the thought becomes an obession as it gets nearer to closing time. If it is your own party the remedy is in your own hands, and during the war I succeeded in convincing a great number of friendly Americans that it was an old English custom to knock off lunch in time to get round to a pub; I often hope it did not cause too much misunderstanding when they were lunching with other limeys and said at the end of lunch 'And where are we going for our pint?' But very often you get away from other people's parties barely in time.

These are the occasions when you need to know not only the shortest road to the nearest pub but, very often, the nearest pub that is not within sight of the place where you lunched or dined. Some hosts, not appreciating the unique qualities of draught beer, might feel slighted if they saw you plunging into a pub as they tipped the doorman for letting them get into their car; they might wonder why you refused the third brandy if you were still in need of drink. So you may have to become a furtive frequenter, very glad to know of a pub round the corner or an entrance up the mews.

This is a large subject and I cannot claim to have mastered it. I have my own resorts: for instance the White Lion from Claridge's, the Red Lion from the Dorchester, Ward's off the Strand from the Savoy (or the Public Bar of the Coal Hole if you come out at the back). But each of us must make his own list of bolt-holes according to his own needs. It is not only restaurants that evoke them, but offices, museums, churches, concert-halls, airline terminals, even the houses of hospitable but wine-fancying friends. Most of these have the advantage that no host comes out when you do so you can make a bee-line for the pub. You can leave the British Museum and scurry off to the Plough in Little Russell Street or the Bull and Mouth in what they now call Bloomsbury Way, and you can drown the taste of the Foreign Office at the Red Lion just across the road. As for the houses of your friends, if your host follows you out and meets you again in the pub, the laugh is on him rather than on you.

From this point of view, the more pubs there are the better. But the pub-goer's map of London was shrinking steadily long before the bombing began. If you find a really modest pub, old-fashioned, unaffected, small, where you are given a welcome and can quickly get served, you may be almost sure that it is slated for demolition, though it may have been reprieved by the war.

Rebuilding and Redundancy

This great subject of the vanishing of pubs deserves a special word, and it is one on which I must admit that the sentimental pub-goer like Ardizzone and myself is often opposed to all the interests—brewer, Bench, publican, and sometimes staff. All these people, for their different reasons, would rather have one modern pub than three old-fashioned ones. We on the other hand would, as a general rule, trade one modern pub for one old-fashioned one, let alone three.

The brewers want pubs that do a big trade, and from their simple economic standpoint they are right; it is more profitable to make people fill one pub than to let them drink in any of three. The licensing justices often seem not to like pubs at all; the fewer the better is their motto, and though you can never get leave to open a new pub in an old area it is very easy to get leave to close one down. The publicans of today are apt to be progressive characters who are working their way up from pub to pub instead of settling down in one and making it their home, and they know that the better their trade the better their chance of getting the brewery to give them a bigger house. The staff like the coming-and-going of a busy place and of course they often get greater comfort in a modern house. Maybe some of the customers like the tendency too, but I doubt whether anybody has ever taken their view.

Of the two dangers, Rebuilding and Redundancy, the worse is of course Redundancy. For many years now the magistrates and the brewers who own the licences have been agreeing that certain neighbourhoods have too many pubs and picking out the least profitable to be closed down. The brewers compensate themselves out of the increased takings of the surviving pubs, and the magistrates beam as they rub another plague-spot off their maps. The people who looked upon the condemned house as their local have to put up with it. It is all rather reminiscent of slave-dealing days.

However, the Redundancy movement had done its worst (or maybe its best, for I am trying not to be prejudiced about this issue) some years ago, and the next great danger was Rebuilding. Not dissimilar in its motives, this aimed at replacing the noisome tavern of old superstition by the modern café-pub, clean, light, airy, spacious, where, in the reformer's dream, the Man could bring his wife and family to sit at small tables and drink soft drinks if they so desired. It was left to the sentimentalists like Ardizzone and me to reply that the modern pub may be better but the old-fashioned pub was nicer; that we do not want to sit at small tables and pay a waiter to bring us our drinks; that the Man seemed to have no scruples about bringing his wife to the old-fashioned pub, and as for the children, we all go to the pubs to get away from them; in short, that we have seldom known a pub to be improved by rebuilding, and we have known plenty to be spoiled.

Here again let me try to be impartial. In the days of the real gin-palaces, the flash cellars, and the evil dens by the waterfront, demolition with or without rebuilding may have been a good thing. For myself I have never come across those places; I have read about them in books, and I sometimes wonder whether they were as bad then as they were written up to be; one reads very odd things in books even now. But by the time I started using the London pubs there was little prosperous vice to be found; the most you would encounter was a rather melancholy decay. Social progress had drawn the blood away from the really villainous pub, but the demolition and the rebuilding went on. It was an added misfortune that the modernisation movement reached its peak in years when contemporary standards in architecture and furnishing were so bad. The epoch of light oak and tile-topped tables, with outbreaks of chromium plate and three-legged tubular stools, gave us bad replacements for the mahogany and etched glass of the typical Victorian pub, to say nothing of the dark gleaming mellowness of the house that had not changed for a hundred years. One felt positively grateful to pub-holders like Youngers and Henekeys whose antique style was at least quiet and restful to the eye.

No part of London has been more thoroughly rebuilt than that surrounding the lower end of Horseferry Road, where from the Lutyens flats to the big office blocks on the Embankment there is hardly a building that was there fifteen years ago. I happened to make a round of the pubs in that neighbourhood on August Bank Holiday 1936, when the demolition was going on, and I never visited more cheerful pubs. They were singing and dancing in the Westminster Arms, there was an accordion playing in the Wellington, which was the only house left standing in Page Street; they were merry under the gaslight in the Clarence, which was the only building left in the block. At the Paviours, otherwise known as the Rat Hole, they were serving in the kitchen and everybody was having a fine time.

I went round again on August Bank Holiday 1937. I found no signs of Bank Holiday anywhere, and the Wellington and the Clarence had gone. You will still find the Westminster and the Paviours among the stately though not inspiring architecture of Marsham Court and Westminster Gardens, rising nine storeys over your head; the Westminster has gradually regained a friendly local feeling, but the Paviours is all strip lighting and pin-tables, and I think the Rat Hole was a nicer pub.

The transition phase of 'Business as Usual' amongst the demolition and the rebuilding was the only good thing about the modernisation of the pubs. It has always been an axiom among drinkers that the Law compels a pub to go on serving, on however small a scale, with the penalty of losing the licence if it closes for a single day. This seemed to lapse long before the war, when buildings with deep foundations closed whole streets and sometimes the pub reappeared on the other side of the road, but the tradition went on. I remember drinking at the old Queen's Head in Denman Street (the one with the mountainous and motherly Queenie behind the lunch-bar) as foot after foot was lost to the builders until their ladders finally met practically over your head; and it was more fun than drinking at the Queen's Head now. The Adelphi Hotel went on serving beer throughout the roaring reconstruction that took away the Adam terrace and gave London an eyesore instead, and there was a delight in threading a way through the scaffolding and finding the couple of casks on a trestle that kept the licence alive. But the classic case of rebuilding was probably the Two Chairmen in South Bruton Mews, and perhaps I may re-tell it even though it happened a year or two before the war.

When I first knew it this was a creeper-clad corner pub in the crooked mews behind Berkeley Square, and the square was probably still much as it was when it was laid out in 1698. The pub was small and pleasant, with a private bar served through a hatch, and outside it a sort of glorified bulkhead in which a cobbler worked, this being famous as London's Smallest Shop. Then came the shadow of Berkeley Square House. Demolition began on all sides—the thrilling business of pick and shovel, lorry and crane, always so absorbing to watch though so often disastrous in final result. For a time the pub prospered, crowded with thirsty labourers washing the brick-and-mortar dust out of their throats, until one evening it ceased to be. The road to it was barred, for this was a radical rebuilding and the very thoroughfare was being diverted; South Bruton Mews was changing to a new Bruton Lane. For a spell the old fascia-board still showed over the hoardings, but I thought the pub had gone.

Then one day a wooden hut arose at the end of a causeway, built out on piles over the excavations that probed far down into the soil. It looked like a builders' hut until men crawled along it, scaled the roof, and hoisted the old original Toby sign.

From that time onwards, throughout the rebuilding, the Two Chairmen plied its trade. It was hard to get to sometimes, as the building rose around it and the blackboard saying PUB—➤ pointed to a narrow path of planks laid in deep mire; but at the end of the path was the little shack with a few barrels and a darts-board. It was a nice place to have a drink on one's way home.

Then came another change. The shack vanished and the pub reappeared in a new place, as part of the ground floor of the massive new block. Inside it was large and airy and unadorned, outside there was no brewer's sign. It was an unconventional but not a bad pub.

But the changes went on. Outside came Neon lights and a signboard showing the two chairmen carrying their sedan chair, but a sedan chair constructed on so novel a principle that not Hercules and Samson could have carried it without spilling its occupant out. The inside too began to sprout; giant beams that rang hollow to the knuckle, medieval doors, Tudor roses on the walls. A little pamphlet appeared, complete with long s'es that looked much more like italic f's, giving the history of the house from the time of Charles II but not going into the little matter of the rebuilding and change of address under George VI.

Time heals all things, and after ten years I can look upon the Two Chairmen as quite a nice comfortable Truman house in a convenient spot. But I should not choose to go to it if I could still find the old house standing a little further up the mews.

Not all rebuilding is so extreme; the York Minster in Dean Street was rebuilt so painlessly that you can forget it has been, and some of the new houses are very nice. Especially the smaller ones, like the Old Rose in Monck Street and the King's Head in Marylebone, to name two that happen to appeal to me. But it is depressing to visit the pubs that were pioneers of modern ideas in the thirties, such as the Plough at Clapham, one of the first and most-publicised examples of the café-tavern, and see how melancholy they look. It is quite refreshing to go from this fading enlightenment to the Alexandra Hotel across the road and revel in the unabashed splendours of an Edwardian saloon.

I must not harp unduly on this question of rebuilding, which has not been a live issue since the war. But it is hard to forget the painful experience of the past—the awful moment of apprehension when the landlord of some nice, neglected old pub told you the brewers were going to rebuild, and the strain of indulging his pride in the hideous plans. It would be easier if one could feel sure that the glowing future of national recovery would not see the fell work starting all over again.

Names and Signs

Failing the ability to rebuild, the people who own pubs (and that is mostly the brewers) are taking an interest in the decoration of the pubs that they have got now. This is another controversial subject and I had better avoid it; Ardizzone and I share the conviction—so strong as to be almost furious—that the best thing the artist can do to the pub is to leave it alone, and that no amount of design, no amusing textiles and ingenious furnishings, can get as good a result as you find in many a rather dark bar that gleams softly with the reflections from well-scrubbed pewter and well-polished glass. The tortuous interiors of the old houses have a charm that you can hardly recreate, and nothing that I have seen in the exhibitions is likely to give me so much pleasure as the gilt-etched mirrors, crowned by eagles, at the Spread Eagle in Grosvenor Road, the glass shutters, with their oak-leaf pattern, at the Royal Oak near Eaton Square, the fantastic ceiling of the Black Horse in Rathbone Place; and it would take a lot of modern design to create an interior so imposing as the faded Palladian of Mooney's in the Strand. There is scope for design in the small things of the pub, such as the tankards, but if they want to make new designs instead of studying the shapes that have served well in the past, let them begin by realising that the important thing about a tankard is that if it spills a little, or is not quite filled, you shan't lose too much of the beer you have paid for, and that means (and a fig for aesthetics) that it should not be too wide in proportion to its height, and above all that it should not be too wide at the top.

Turning to the brighter side and avoiding becoming too peevish and staying so too long, it is pleasant to see that one of the results of the new interest in design and decoration is a re-emergence of the signboard bearing the name of the house. For a long time the brewers seemed to regard the pub as no more than a free hoarding on which to advertise their wares, and although you could see from a mile off whose beer it sold, you had to be a detective to find out what the house itself was called. There is some value in proclaiming the brew, certainly; sometimes it serves as an invitation and other times as a warning, and it is a pity that some of the rebuilt houses go to the other extreme and it is hard to find out whose beer they sell even when you go inside. But the forest of Watneys and Charringtons and Taylor Walkers all over London grows very depressing, and it is good to see that artists are being commissioned to paint new sign-boards, and that from the less fancy ones you can actually learn the name.

After all, the names are part of the appeal of the pubs. It would be far easier not to go to them if they were all called just Barclays or Whitbreads as it might be Lyons and the ABC. The most ordinary pubs have names evoking history, patriotism, legend, and romance.

My own locals are in no way exceptional but their names are the Windsor Castle, the Pineapple, the Duke of Cambridge, the Prince of Orange, the Phoenix and the Bag o' Nails. Some neighbourhoods have them strung out like a roll-call. Albany Street, for instance, is not an inspiring thoroughfare, but as you walk up it you are kept going by the pub names. The Queen's Head and Artichoke, the Cape of Good Hope, the Chester Arms, the Windsor Castle, the Victory, the Prince George of Cumberland, and the Crown and Anchor give you impetus to traverse the long blank stretch that leads to the York and Albany facing the Park at the top.

There is something for everybody in the names. To counter the aristocracy of the Portmans and Devonshires and Westminsters (with a Marquis of Westminster amongst them to show that it is no parvenu pub) are the trades—Bricklayers, Masons, Plumbers, Coachmakers, Turners. There are the East India Arms, the China Ship, the Steam Packet, the Ticket Porter, and many others that pay tribute to local occupations present or past; there are endless reminders of transport by chairmen, footmen, horse, coach, ferry; there is an exotic garden of Orange Trees and Lemon Trees and a heraldic zoo full of Red Lions, White Harts, and Unicorns; there are Turk's Heads and Blackamoor's Heads, Golden Crosses, Silver Crosses, and Shades; Lord Nelsons and Duke of Wellingtons; sporty titles like the Champion and romantic titles like the Royal Pair; there is a Hole in the Wall, a Hog in the Pound, a Hero of Maida, a Hero of Switzerland, and a Hero of Waterloo; there are curious combinations of lions and dolphins and cocks and green men, which inspire the antiquarians to some of their finest flights.

Personally I must confess to a shade of scepticism about some of these derivations. The Elephant and Castle seems to me just as likely a name to choose for your pub as the Infanta of Castile, and the Bull and Mouth not much less likely a title than the Boulogne Mouth. As for the Goat and Compasses, I think it is sheer effrontery to insist that it really meant the God Encompasseth Us; who would ever call a pub by an unpronounceable name like that?

I used to stay in a small hotel in Paris called the Hotel de l'Univers et du Portugal, but nobody ever invented a theory that the person who named the hotel did not regard Portugal as part of the universe. It seemed obvious that the hotel had once been two even smaller hotels and they had combined. No doubt a small inn called the Goat (a not uncommon title) combined with a small inn called the Compasses (the sign of a craft) and somebody else saw the name and thought it a good one to use on his own house, and so it spread. After all, there is no rhyme or reason about what you can call a pub.

These amalgamations must account for a lot of the poetry of pub names: the Green Man and French Horn, the Horse and Dolphin, the Six Bells and Bowling Green. Of course, there are obvious pairings like the George and Dragon, the Lamb and Flag, the Cock and Lion, the Bear and Staff, whose significance even I can understand. But I feel that to frame a theory that will combine the Horse with the Dolphin or force the White Horse into the Bower is probably a waste of time; and I wonder how many legends of the Intrepid Fox that took the hunt through Wardour Street might have grown up if that admirable pub did not still display a plaque relating its title to the Westminster election of 1780 and the victory of Charles James Fox.

The Drink Question

Before we cut the cackle and get to the pictures I should say one word on the practical question of what to drink in your pub when you have found it, assuming that it is not your own local and that you have not learnt by experience what they keep best.

It would seem impertinent to write about a subject so much open to personal taste if it were not that so many pub-goers never attempt to plumb the resources of the pubs. I have met life-long bitter-drinkers who thought that Burton was a brand rather than a brew, and old habitués of the Saloon Bar who asked whether old-and-mild came out of one tap or two. That is the only excuse for the notes on drinks that appear in irritating detail in the Glossary at the end of this book.

I am concerned here with draught beer, for this is on the whole the staple drink in the pubs, and the drink that varies more than any other from brewery to brewery and from pub to pub. It is therefore the drink about which the pub-goer can best be knowledgeable. A bottled Bass (to mention only one brand) should not vary very much wherever you get it, a branded Scotch should vary even less, and wine in pubs is, speaking generally, a thing to avoid. But the draught beers take a bit of knowing, and they repay study even after the war.

The war has ironed out many differences and narrowed the field of choice. The days of Zoning are over, but the weakening of beer all round has taken the edge off many fine distinctions. Personally I find that I can drink brews that I could not drink before, partly because their rivals have got worse too and partly because the weakening has taken away the worst of the taste. The merging of breweries goes on, and it takes some time to realise that the name you see over the house is not always the name that goes on the casks. But if the brewery is less important, the landlord is all the more so. The keeping and serving of the beer make almost more difference now than the brewing, and the quality in any pub can change with a new landlord or even a new girl behind the bar.

The drinks that you could once expect to find on draught in a pub included mild ale, bitter, Burton or Scotch ale, stout, strong ale or barley wine, and sometimes lager, cider, spirits, sherry and port; you would not expect to find all these in one house but you could hope for a fairly wide choice. Even before the war draught stout was beginning to go the way of porter, and several breweries did not brew Burton during the warmer months. Oddly enough, both these tendencies have shown signs of being reversed. Burton, after disappearing completely during the war, has begun to come back; there is more of it about in the winter, and Barclays for one brew it all the year round. Draught stout owes its revival mainly to Guinness, who are now sending it out in ten-gallon metal containers which stand on the bar. The trouble about draught Guinness used to be in keeping it and serving it, and the container keeps it under pressure and makes it easier to serve— though a good barmaid can still make it better and get more into the glass. Despite its price draught Guinness seems to sell readily enough all over London; I have seen half-a-dozen containers in a row at the Horns in Kennington, and the smaller houses can keep one at a time. Mackesons are doing the same thing, and I have even seen Simonds's bitter served in this way.

Anything that makes for more variety, and especially for more draught stout, is all to the good, but I do hope that the trade will soon evolve some nicer name for the novel device. 'Metal container' is hardly worthy to take its place among the pins and firkins and spiles and spigots that make up the vocabulary of the pubs.

Even nowadays, the different breweries and the different brews provide for most tastes. My own fancy (leaving price out of it) is for Guinness's stout on draught, Younger's Scotch ale, Benskin's bitter, Barclay's mild ale; but old-and-mild is usually a safe drink when you can get it. Ardizzone is a bitter-drinker by conviction. The next person will have different tastes again.

As for prices, that is a subject on which it is impossible to write. It was fairly easy ten years ago, when prices were stable and the famous penny-on-the-pint tax had come and gone again. In those days I used to have little sympathy with older drinkers who were always remembering that whisky once cost three-and-sixpence a bottle and beer was twopence a pint. Now, as I part with my money, I myself find it hard not to talk about the days when Guinness on draught cost tenpence a pint at Mooney's and the standard price for mild ale was fivepence in the Public Bar. At fourpence a glass or fourpence-halfpenny a half-pint in the Saloon, beer was a cheap drink. I remember a friend of mine, a lifelong actor who had become a journalist, telling me of his surprise and delight when he found that in his new world of beer-drinkers he could go into a pub with a friend, order two drinks, put down a shilling, and get change.

The price of beer today seems fantastic, but there is no knowing whether before this book comes out it will have gone up again. Periodically it looks as though it had gone out of reach; publicans begin to worry, in small houses you find you have a bar to yourself and in big houses you see the barmaids sitting down at nine o'clock. But what has most amazed me has been the frequency with which you see people ordering the more expensive drinks—filling bottled strong ale up with bitter to make a pint and using light ale as a chaser for short drinks. Only this morning I saw a Sunday drinker popping a gin into his pint and felt as I used to feel when I heard somebody ordering draught champagne.

*   *   *

Finally, I must apologise to people who are mostly interested in the historical connections and literary associations of the pubs, for this book has little to do with them. There have been excellent books dealing with these subjects, but the ravages of time and fire and modernisation have forced them to be written mainly in the past tense. Most of the pubs even of Dickens's time have disappeared, and it is no part of my purpose to guide people to office blocks in new thoroughfares where the pleasure of knowing that there used to be a coaching tavern has to make up for the fact that you can't get a drink.

The pubs with genuine histories have usually been rebuilt, have sometimes changed their name and often changed their site. It is true that one takes more pleasure in a drink at say the Union Arms in Panton Street for the knowledge that Tom Cribb, the Champion of England, did keep a house of that name in that street, but it is not necessary to believe that Tom Cribb would recognise it if he came back. It is nice to know that the Town of Ramsgate at the corner of Wapping Old Stairs was where the mob caught Judge Jeffreys in 1688, disguised as a sailor and trying to escape abroad; but I suspect the house looked different then, and it was certainly called the Red Cow. In my own time I have seen too many pubs rebuilt and even moved, taking their historical associations with them, to feel much confidence in the spell of history. There are a few surviving pubs of undoubted authenticity, like the George in Southwark (1676), the Cheshire Cheese off Fleet Street (which is as it was rebuilt after the Great Fire), and I believe the Devereux off Essex Street, the original Grecian coffee-house; but with most venerable houses I am always prepared to meet some older drinker who remembers when they were rebuilt.

The old inns have survived better on the outskirts than in the centre, as might be expected. The Spaniards on Hampstead Heath is the pick of them, with its toll-house, its garden, and an interior that really feels old, but there are others, like Jack Straw's Castle, the Flask at Highgate, and even the Old Gate House there, which looks so obviously faked-up that one tends not to give it a second thought, though I believe the reconstruction is entirely superficial and the inside is as it was in Dick Turpin's time. But mostly you are lucky if the houses with historic names can show an old fireplace, a signboard, even a few tankards and a coaching-horn, to remind you of the days of their fame, and personally I am more conscious of continuity in a house like the Hole in the Wall under the arches at Waterloo, which cannot have been there more than a hundred years but looks to me as though it had hardly changed in all that time.

Associations certainly add to the pleasure one takes in strange pubs, so long as they are still pubs and you can get a drink in them. From this point of view a live dog is better than a dead lion. The people who use a pub as their local are very often concerned far less with past glory than with present comfort, and there is no denying that the oldest taverns are usually much more comfortable for the patron than the ones they plan now.

But this book does not claim to be a history, any more than it is a sociological survey. Ardizzone and I have followed our own fancy and recalled the things that we ourselves enjoyed. We can only ask other pub-goers to overlook transgressions, make exceptions for their own locals whenever we are wrong, and take the book as a modest tribute to all the locals where we have had so many pleasant times.

THE REGULARS

EVERY pub is somebody's local and every one has its regulars. They may be lunch-time regulars who work near by, or after-supper regulars who would hardly know the place during the day, or six o'clock regulars who look in for a quick one on the way home from work and regularly miss two or three trains. There are West-End pubs where business men spend their evenings so regularly that their wives ring up for them and the barmaid has to send them home. But the most genuine regulars are to be found in the small neighbourhood houses, just round the corner from where they live.

You see them ensconced in the corner by the partition, deep in conversation with the landlady when you come in. The conversation is deep enough to survive interruptions, and the landlady will serve you, exchange a few words, and then return to the corner, lower her voice, and carry on where she left off. The real regular is one of the family. There is nothing he does not know about what happens in the house.

As a regular myself, I have heard more about the affairs of licensed houses than I know about most of my friends. I have followed the career of a landlady's daughter from childhood to marriage, with photographic illustrations, without ever seeing the girl. I have heard another landlady's suspicions of the best barmaid they ever had, ending with 'She as good as admitted she made money when she wasn't working, and what are you to make of that?'. On the other hand I have listened to the confidences of a discharged barmaid in a West-End dive, who had called to settle accounts with the manager. 'He's hiding in the Gentlemen's, the dirty rat, but I'll get him if I have to sit here all night'.

Nothing much is demanded of the regular except to come regularly and show himself interested in the pub's affairs. He need not even drink very much. Most of the regulars are leisurely, even reluctant drinkers. They make a half-pint last a surprisingly long time.

The Regulars at the Hero

Of course, this business of having regulars cuts both ways. There are houses where you feel embarrassed if you are not a regular, and even houses where the occasional visitor has difficulty in getting served. The beer shortage has aggravated this feeling; xenophobia flourishes in times of short supplies. But in general a very few visits will get you on good terms, and even if you are quite unknown the presence of the regulars in their corners is a tranquillising influence on the house. This is especially so on Sunday mornings, when the regular customers muster in full force. The Sunday morning walk, bringing you to the doors of the local just as they open at twelve or twelve-thirty, is one of the great institutions of the ordinary man. The two gentlemen pacing back from the Warwick Castle in the frontis-piece (obviously on a Sunday morning) are as good regulars as the two in the Hero of Maida in the picture facing p. 22.

Peaceful and inoffensive (for the most part), the regulars would seem to have no enemies, but malice has not passed them by. They were the chief victims of the bombing as well as of the rebuilding craze. Wherever a nice old-fashioned pub has been pulled down and turned into a cross between a road-house and a sanatorium, wherever a bombed site has taken the place of a pub, it is the regulars who suffer. Like fish out of water they try to adapt themselves to a new environment and fail. The more regular they have been, the harder it is for them to go elsewhere. It is a sad ending to a modest and not altogether useless career.

BARMAIDS OLD AND NEW

For a long time I tried to attribute the decline of barmaids as a factor in the attractiveness of pubs to my own increasing age, but I am beginning to fear that it is an objective fact.

My pub-going days date only from the twenties, and no doubt older drinkers will tell me that the barmaids of that period had already lost their glory. Yet they had survivors. The ample bosom clad in black satin, the artfully-wrought pile of peroxide hair, the fingers all covered with diamonds (as W. W. Jacobs put it), lasted until my time. These were the barmaids of tradition, the confidential barmaids to whom the customers whispered over the bar, the haughty barmaids who could freeze the insubordinate with a look, the dominating barmaids who could quell a riot with a word, the tolerant barmaids who could listen unmoved to talk of the most doubtful description and then turn in a flash into highly virtuous barmaids who would order the loose talker outside. And when they ordered anybody outside, he would go.

These massive and powerful personalities were, it is true, a survival. The between-the-wars barmaid tended to be younger, slimmer, smarter; but she was still an attraction. Some pubs made a speciality of them, and some barmaids attained a following of their own. I remember when a new barmaid at the Tivoli brought a lot of familiar faces from the Queen's.

But they had become a rarity even in 1939. In general, the better-looking the barmaid, the less long-lived. If they did not quarrel with the manager they quarrelled with the manageress. They were here today and gone tomorrow. And when they went, they seemed to go completely. Perhaps they got married; at any rate they did not go where the customers could follow them, and their successors seemed to get less attractive every time.

The war completed the process. Few London barmaids are London girls, and when the black-out began most of them seemed to go home. A few lingered until the call-up got them, and that finished it. Even the coming of the Americans, who attracted to

Barmaids Old and New

London so many girls of types we had not seen before, did not rock the pubs. By 1942 sex-appeal was no more of an element in drinking in London than it is in New York.

The end of the war has made little difference; whatever the glamour girls of today are doing, they do not seem to be going into the licensed trade. I should be surprised to find any pub-goer who could lay his hand on his heart and name three houses that he frequents on account of the beauty, intelligence, and wit of the young person behind the bar.

Personally I put my faith in the old people nowadays. At one time it was true that the better-looking the barmaid, the better you got served. The barmaid who was there to attract men knew how to do it; she was anxious to please. If anybody was slow and rude and bungling it was apt to be the poor old thing whose feet hurt her and whose mind had long ago turned against men. After one or two rebuffs from these it was a pleasure to go, say, to the Spread Eagle in Oxford Street, where the two dizzy blondes both sprang forward to serve you as soon as you opened the door.

Now the tables are turned. Generalisations are always dangerous, I know, and there may be lovely young barmaids who reserve their interest for their younger customers, but I have not seen them doing it. So far as my experience goes, if you want to be well looked after and well served, you are lucky if you can find a barmaid on the far side of fifty, who likes serving people and knows that the way you handle the beer-pulls can make a lot of difference to what you get in the glass.

THE SALOON LOUNGE

WITH their instinct for social distinctions, their morbid passion for what Americans call self-stratification, the English have divided their pubs up into the greatest possible number of compartments. A London pub can have a Saloon Lounge, Saloon Bar, Private Bar, Public Bar, Jug-and-Bottle, and Ladies' Bar, to say nothing of such refinements as Wine Bars, Lunch Bars, Buffet Bars, and Dives.

Let us start, as is fitting, with the most respectable of all the standard categories—the Saloon Lounge.

The Lounge is standard to the extent that many pubs have one, but it is a refinement on the Saloon Bar. It shows, therefore, that the pub possessing one has aspirations. It caters for a class of people who want something a little better even than the Saloon Bar. In pubs that have both, the Lounge implies sitting at tables, having drinks fetched by waiters, and tipping. The extra expense of tipping accounts for the greater grandeur of the Lounge.

All the same, the Lounge is going out, or at least ceasing to be a refinement on the Saloon. Few modern pubs have both, for the modern Lounge has the same advantages and the same drawbacks as the modern Saloon. An acre of bare flooring with a strictly rectilinear bar-counter along one side of it hardly justifies the name, even if it is dotted with stream-lined tables and chairs. The Lounge proper belongs to an older order, like first-class on the District Railway. To relish its splendours you must go to the old-established houses where you can hope to find pillars and mirrors and imposing stairs. There is a fine Lounge, with a billiards-room opening off it, at the Railway Hotel in Putney High Street, and there is a real old-world atmosphere about the Lounge at the Salisbury in St. Martin's Lane, with its brass-topped tables, curved horsehair settees, and the artful mirror on the under side of the stairs. But the finest flower of Lounges is the one at the Warrington, which Ardizzone has drawn.

The Warrington is a landmark in Maida Vale, where its fine

The Lounge at the Warrington

building on a commanding corner dominates a whole neighbourhood. Nor has it rested on its laurels and let progress pass it by.
Some years before the war its solid frontage was enlivened by a
lighted sign proclaiming the existence of 'London's Liveliest
Lounge'.

That was a proud boast and an interesting claim, for liveliness
is a quality not encouraged by the licensing Bench, who seem to
think that if you must drink you had better drink *sotto voce*, so to
speak, and such frivolities as music and dancing tend to aggravate
the crime. But the Warrington did its best to justify it inside as
well as out by modernising the decoration of its historic lounge.

This Lounge has a magnificent staircase, heavy, old-fashioned,
imposing. The mere sight of it makes you think of Edwardian
revelry, of well-nourished bookmakers and stout ladies in cart-
wheel hats, of feather boas and parasols and malacca canes, of
dogskin gloves and big cigars. Until the redecoration the whole
Lounge shared something of this air of the days when it did not
need to claim to be the Liveliest Lounge.

Luckily the staircase remained. It looked a bit incongruous at
first, amongst the modern furniture and the modern custom that
the furniture brought with it. But there is a vitality in these
survivals that you cannot altogether drive out with three-legged
tubular stools, and the atmosphere of Maida Vale itself still favours
the Edwardian side. Now that the modernisation is ten years old
or so, it seems to matter less. The first thing you notice is the
staircase and the arches, and against that background the flashiest
of present-day types begins to look more and more as though he
had a dog-cart waiting outside.

THE SALOON BAR

ONE of the most fascinating things about the pubs is the way they are carved up by interior partitions into the most unexpected and fantastic shapes. It is often quite startling to look up at the ceiling and realise that all these compartments, varying so widely in their geography and in their social significance, are merely sketched on the ground plan of a simple rectangular space. Pull down the partitions, and instead of a complicated series of bars you would just have a medium-sized room.

In a lot of modernised pubs they have pulled down the partitions and all the mystery has gone. But in the older houses the Saloon Bar may be approached down a corridor running the whole length of the house, with other bars opening off it, as it is at Grafton's in Strutton Ground or the Three Nuns in Aldgate, or it may have its entrance round the corner or up the mews, as at the White Lion in Brook Street or the Golden Lion in King Street. It may even be up a few stairs, as at the Allsopp House (now called Allen's) in Marylebone Road. The Saloon is apt to be discreet; often everything possible is done, even to the provision of glass shutters in the bar itself, to save the Saloon habitué from realising that he is under the same roof as his social inferiors in the Public Bar, and to prevent their seeing that he is having one too.

For the Saloon is more expensive than the Public Bar. The amount of the tax on social superiority varies, but even if it is only a penny on the pint it is enough to make the Saloon the bar of the employers, the officials, the managing class; unless of course the house has an even fancier bar.

Like everything else in the pubs, the characteristics of the Saloon vary from pub to pub. It may be the biggest bar in the house or the smallest. You can find enormous Saloons as in the Windsor Castle at Victoria or the Horseshoe in Tottenham Court Road, small crowded Saloons as at the Prince of Orange in Howick Place or the Punch Bowl in Farm Street or the Red Lion off Pall

The Saloon Bar at the Prince
Alfred

Mall, cavernous architectural Saloons as at the Black Horse in Rathbone Place or at the Prince Alfred, which Ardizzone has drawn.

But the Saloon Bar has certain common characteristics wherever you find it. It is in the Saloon that you get (according to the period when the house was last done up) the ferns in great brass pots, the bevelled mirrors, the reproductions of 'Popularity' and 'Derby Day' or the pencil drawings of the brewery's other pubs, the coloured caricature of the landlord, the talking parrot, the pin-tables, the juke-boxes, the chromium-plated beer pulls, the pewter tankards. And talking about tankards, it is only in the Saloon Bar that I have ever met those half-pint tankards with false bottoms and bell tops which succeed in giving the impression that half-a-pint is quite a considerable drink. There would not be much demand for them in the Public Bar.

Finally, the Saloon Bar is the headquarters of the landlord himself. It is here that he chats to the habitués and allows them to buy him drinks, whether he actually consumes the drinks or not. It is here, too, that dalliance with the barmaids is practised in the diminishing number of houses where barmaids are dallied with. The Saloon Bar is comfort, superiority, elegance, and the feeling of doing yourself well; and very pleasant that feeling can be.

There are, however, houses here and there that have no Saloon Bar.

THE PUBLIC BAR

THE Public Bar is the cheapest and most plebeian part of the house. There are no waiters, no hospital collecting-boxes, no pin-tables (though you may find shove-ha'penny and darts); you can bring your lunch with you and eat it without undue comment, as you could hardly do in the average Saloon. You pay nothing for decoration so the price of beer is down to rock-bottom. In the Public Bar you see more ale sold than bitter, and pints are less the exception than the rule.

Indeed, one of the dangers of writing about the London pubs is the danger of sentimentally glorifying the Public Bar.

However, the foregoing pages about the Saloon Lounge and Saloon Bar have tried to explain the merits of these higher-priced compartments. All I can say is that their gilded luxury and almost lascivious attractions make the change to the simple pleasures of the Public Bar all the more enjoyable. After all, you can always change back.

Social distinctions being what they are in England, the Public Bar is by no means open to all. There are many Public Bars where any patron who is too obviously not dressed as a labourer is regarded with distrust. His presence is resented by the patrons as well as by the management, on the natural grounds that he is a person who can afford to use the Saloon Bar and therefore his reason for going elsewhere must presumably be either curiosity or parsimony. Both are motives justly despised in the Public Bar.

Besides, the Public side has not forgotten what it suffered during the darts craze before the war. The managements were not quick enough in putting darts boards into the Saloon, so some of the most unsuitable elements from that side drained into the four-ale bar, talking in those high penetrating voices that are so distressing to anybody not thoroughly conditioned to them, and the locals sat in hopeless apathy while young women with blood-red fingernails threw doubles with hard-boiled charm. That does not happen now but it has left its scars, and any unlikely visitor to the

The Public Bar at the George

Public is apt to set them wondering whether some new menace is on the way.

As I have never been a labourer I must confess that my own experience of Public Bars is limited compared with my experience of Saloons. But there are pubs where it is made very easy for you to go into the cheap side; for instance, those where they don't serve mild in the Saloon, or those where the Saloon is often so crowded that you can't get served at all. In these matters the start is all-important. Once you have been in a few times you can go whenever you like.

Then there are the houses that have no Saloon. These can be quite big houses like the Victoria Stores where the whole of the licensed area is given up to one partition-less bar, all Public and all cheap. Incidentally, this bar is as spacious and airy, with as much sitting-room and as many tables, as most of the rebuilt, modern-minded, café-style Saloons.

This of course is not a typical one-bar house. To find the genuine Saloon-less London pub that might be a country pub you must search in the back streets and the mews. You will find them in many parts of London, rich as well as poor; in fact there is no likelier neighbourhood than the little villages that lie behind the big houses of an earlier age, when the pubs were planned on the assumption that people who wanted to be better than their fellows would not go to the pubs at all. Of the four surviving houses in the nest of little streets that lies between Belgrave Square and Hobart Place, three have only one bar.

It is not a matter of size; the smallest interior can have a cubicle carved out of it in which they charge more. And there is plenty of room for a cheap side in many West-End pubs that, I am sad to say, have no Public Bar.

THE JUG-AND-BOTTLE BAR

SOME progressive thinkers talk as though the pubs were a relic of the darkest ages of British civilisation, on a par with back-to-back cottages and child labour in the mines. They are frequently the same thinkers who point to Hogarth's Gin Lane and Beer Alley as examples of the evils of intemperance, though what Hogarth was trying to do was to illustrate the merits of beer as opposed to gin. But however stoutly these thinkers are to be resisted on many points, it is hard not to give them best over the Jug-and-Bottle Bar.

The Jug-and-Bottle (or Bottle-and-Jug) has a taint of furtiveness that is not shared by the rest of the pub. There is a sort of sneaking assumption that whilst it would be disgraceful to be seen drinking in a pub, it is consistent with respectability to use the Bottle-and-Jug. The theory, presumably, is that in this bar you are buying for your husband and not for yourself, but some of the customers give you the impression that if they have got a husband, he won't get much of what they buy.

This hypocritical outlook is further emphasised by the shutters or jalousies that usually fence this under-handed bar, and by such weak pretences as bringing back the empties in attaché-cases or taking away the bottles in paper containers not marked with the name of the pub. On the assumption that you are unwilling to be seen carrying beer in the street, I have known barmen to wrap bottles in paper without being asked, even though the practical result might be that in carrying them you kept a firm grip on the paper whilst the bottle fell to the ground.

One stage beyond the Jug-and-Bottle is the Off-Licence, which is the pub shorn of all its sociability, masquerading as a shop. But the Off-Licence has one important quality that the Jug-and-Bottle has not. Usually it flourishes where there is no pub. It is not a question of choice between going into the Jug-and-Bottle and going into one of the bars, but of choice between going to the Off-Licence and going without.

The Jug and Bottle at the
Green Man

All that can be said against the practice of buying or ordering drinks for home consumption has been said long ago by G. K. Chesterton, who weighted his case a shade unfairly with duchesses and dressing-rooms. It is possible to drink at home without hypocrisy, and nowadays it is very useful to know that you can get a drink at home if you can't get one out.

This is where the pubs are most apt to fail you. It is not only that few of them still keep a Jug-and-Bottle Bar, for this, like the Ladies' Bar, belongs to an earlier age and few modern pubs have one. The more serious trouble is that so often the pubs cannot provide you with a bottle and cannot even fill your jug.

This is not sheer obstructiveness; it is of course due to the beer shortage which sets in every now and again. When a house has got its quota of beer and worked it out so that it can open for certain hours during the week, it does not like to upset its calculations by parting with beer in bulk. The customers would resent it if they saw anybody carrying off too much in jug or bottle and then they themselves could not get a drink over the bar.

As for bottles, there is a whole new market in them. If you happen to own a quart bottle, stick to it. If you move, take it with you. Shed your books, your pictures, even your clothes, for these things you may hope to replace, but a bottle is a thing you cannot buy. With one bottle you may install yourself as a take-away customer in a new pub; gradually you may insinuate yourself and be trusted with another, until you build up a healthy supply. But without the first bottle you cannot begin to bridge that gap that lies between closing-time and reopening; particularly the long gaps that follow closing-time on Saturday and Sunday nights.

AL FRESCO

OPEN-AIR drinking is very often pleasant even in a climate like ours, but in London it is hard to achieve. On the whole *al fresco* drinking is discouraged; nothing is more familiar than the notice warning you that glasses may not be taken outside. This is due partly to the natural desire of the publican not to lose glasses (and some publicans on the main roads, who cater for the motor-coach trade, could supply interesting figures on that subject), but partly also to respectability, coupled with the general impression that it is illegal to drink on any plot of ground not licensed by the Bench.

In central London, therefore, *al fresco* drinking is largely confined to the children, who may be seen sucking up lemonade on the doorstep of the pub whilst Mum and Dad put away a couple of quick ones inside. Sometimes Mum herself will have Dad fetch her Guinness out to the lobby so that she can keep an eye on little Tommy, but except under the influence of an unusually hot Bank Holiday she is not likely to stray into the street.

There are however pubs where open-air drinking is catered for. There used to be one behind Sloane Street (of all places) where they had tables and benches outside, but it has gone. The Six Bells and Bowling Green in Chelsea has a garden, and many riverside pubs have a balcony. But generally speaking, to drink in the open you must go to the outer suburbs, where there are some famous pubs.

In Barnes, for instance, the Boileau at one end of Castelnau has a large garden, and the Red Lion at the other end has a smaller one which it has done its best to keep as an oasis amongst the encroaching brick-and-mortar. Drinking there can still have a touch of the idyllic, as Ardizzone's drawing shows. There are tables and chairs outside the Green Man at the top of Putney Hill, the Flask at Highgate, and the Windmill on Clapham Common, at which you can drink very pleasantly in the cool of a summer evening. The Gate-House at Barnet (correctly known as the Bell)

46

The Garden at the
Red Lion

has a chestnut tree growing through one bar, so you can drink under the trunk without even going out-of-doors. (It has also the distinction of having the county boundary running through it, as the boundary between Holborn and the City used to run through Fearon's on Holborn Viaduct, so that they had different closing-times at different ends of the bar.) * But the stronghold of *al fresco* drinking is, not unnaturally, Hampstead Heath.

You can drink in the garden at the Bull and Bush, famous in Cockney song; or in the garden at the Spaniards, which is one of the nicest old pubs in London—and there too you can order your drink through a hatch in the wall. You can drink on the verandah at the Vale of Health Hotel, with a peaceful view over the calm water of the pond; but if you have ever had a quiet drink there it was certainly not on an August Bank Holiday night.

Before the war there was never any question of the beer running out, but closing-time came just the same, and in Summer Time it was apt to take you by surprise. You would still be in full swing on the roundabouts, the chairoplanes or the boat-swings when you realised that the pub was just about to close. Then you had to hurl yourself into the press of other people who had been a little quicker at realising the same thing. One does a lot of strenuous things on a fair-ground, but nothing half so exacting and so exciting as getting to the bar, getting served, and getting two well-filled pints back through the crowd at the Vale of Health Hotel.

If closing-time was inexorable, the rule against drinking outside was not. Commonsense asserted itself. At Hampstead on Bank Holiday, as at Mitcham during the Fair, they used to be positively grateful to you if you would take your drink outside and make room for one more pair of elbows in the bar.

---

* Talking of trees, there is one in the Public Bar of the Mitre (or Ye Olde Mitre) in Ely Court, Holborn, though it has been glassed in and I fear it is now dead. This pub claims to date from 1546, and, owing to the Bishop of Ely's extra-territorial rights in the neighbourhood, it still keeps Cambridgeshire licensing hours.

THE MEWS PUB

THE geographical value of pubs in mews, up courts, down
alleys, and in by-streets has already been touched upon
earlier in this book. As for their character when you get to
them, it is obvious that the genuine mews pub is likely to be a
quiet resort rather than a gin-palace or a packed noisy house where
everybody is in a hurry and the cash-register rings all the time.
It attracts not only a quieter type of customer but a quieter type
of landlord. The active go-getter does not stay long in the mews;
nor have the breweries spent much of their money in modernising
mews pubs, where there is little passing custom to attract.

You will find mews pubs all over London from Kensington to
Bloomsbury, some of them patronised by the grand people who
now inhabit mews flats, some completely unspoiled. One of the
nicest mews pubs I ever struck was the White Hart in Brook
Mews North, not far from the Bayswater Road; I felt the real
rewards of exploration when I strayed down that mews and came
into the wide low bar, with hardly a reminder of the twentieth
century in sight. The White Hart is still a nice pub, though the
bombing has robbed it of the screen of buildings that used to
mask it from the street. The little bar at the Stanhope in Wilton
Mews is another typical mews resort, and although they have
enlarged the drinking space they have had the sense to keep the
china beer-pulls intact. The Star Tavern in Belgrave Mews West
has a different clientèle, but it is a fine building that might be a
High Street pub in a country town, with curious iron gates inside
and the approach framed in a most imposing Belgravian arch.
All these three, by the way, sell brews that are not found everywhere in London: Reffell's at the White Hart, Jenner's at the
Stanhope, Fuller's at the Star.

The good mews pubs are legion: one thinks of the Three Tuns
in South Portman Mews, the Grenadier in Old Barrack Yard, the
Guinea in Bruton Place, the Queen's Arms off Queen's Gate
Terrace, the cluster of pubs in Kinnerton Street, to name only a

The Mews Pub

few. And if the mews proper is rare East of Temple Bar there are plenty of alleys, and in the much-bombed hinterland of Fleet Street you can still find a pub round every corner. But to my mind the mews pub *par excellence* is the Dover Castle in Weymouth Mews.

It would take a longer book than this to contain all my memories of the Dover Castle: the days when it was a sleepy, old-fashioned house kept by a quiet old couple (Dad never seen by mortal eye without that bowler hat); the days when it was the local for the commercial radio boys from IBC in Portland Place; the war, the bomb that shook the house to its cellars when it demolished IBC; the coming of Mooney as its landlady, and the emergence of the house as one of the most friendly resorts in the West End.

The Dover Castle has natural advantages; it is in a mews that has still the smell of fodder about it, for Mr. Angell's livery-stables have survived the war, and there is nothing like a pair of saddle-horses or a handsome dog-cart to give an air to a mews pub. But it is Mooney herself who has kept the house old-fashioned but made it bright; has not let the smart people who use it spoil it for the rest; has won the hearts of her regulars by opening on Bank Holidays when every other pub in the neighbourhood is closed, and staying open even when she had no more drink to sell, because, as she says, if she closed where could they all go?

Her reward, apart from giving a lot of pleasure and having a very prosperous house, is fame so great as to rival that of Mooney's Irish Houses, which had a long start. The Dover Castle has no connection with this mighty firm, and Mooney is not even officially called by that name. But a lot of people around the West End, if you said 'Meet you at Mooney's', would go to Weymouth Mews instead of to Oxford Street or Fetter Lane or even the big house in the Strand.

THE WINE HOUSE

WINE is not the drink of the London pubs. That is not to say that no good wine is sold in them, but the wine-drinker, even more than the beer-drinker, has to know where to go.

Some public-houses where they sell also beer and spirits specialise in wine, or at least in sherry and port, which are the staple wines of the pubs. Notable among them are Henekey's houses, which also specialise in a style of antique decoration that is much more pleasing to the eye than antique styles usually are in pubs—or modern styles if it comes to that. Henekey's in Holborn is, I believe, the oldest, with its three-cornered fireplace with no chimney and its rows of cubicles each containing a table and chairs, which give an illusion of privacy not often found in London pubs. The big Henekey's in the Strand has heavy doors swinging on straps, a step down into the bar, and panelling that looks dark with age; but the antique style gives a nice effect even when quite new. There is a house in Marylebone that I used to know as the Angel; it opened as Henekey's no later than 1939, but it is a nice clean job of its kind. And of course there are Henekey's houses that have none of these trappings, such as the Constitution in Churton Street, Pimlico, where their other speciality of draught cider is in greater demand than wine.

Of the other famous chains of wine-houses, Short's are strong in the business quarter; the one at the top of Chancery Lane claims to be London's Oldest Wine-House, but the one near the Gaiety is probably even better known. Yates's Wine Lodges, familiar in the provinces, have one London beach-head in the Strand. There are the Henry Finch houses in Holborn Bars and Whitehall and the Strand; the Bodegas have their head and front in the big house at the corner of Glasshouse Street, but the one in Bedford Street was known to the old laddie actors as the home of the free cheese. Shirreff's famous cellars under the railway bridge on Ludgate Hill were burnt out in the blitz and you can no longer

King's Wine House

drink there with casks for tables and chairs, but they have off-shoots like the one in Margaret Street behind Oxford Circus.And there are wine-houses known to the connoisseurs like Long's in Hanway Street and the sherry house in Baker Street, between Marylebone Road and the Park.

These select resorts must have suffered heavily from war and post-war conditions, but the Wine House proper, such as Ardizzone has drawn, depends little upon connoisseurs. It is at once more respectable and more dissipated than the ordinary pub. People patronise it who would not like the neighbours to see them going into the ordinary Saloon Bar, but when they get there they drink much more seriously. Wine is surprisingly cheap in comparison with its alcoholic content, and a couple of large ports in the Wine House give a much greater sense of comfort than quite a string of bottled beers.

The people who go to the Wine Houses usually need comfort, too. Elderly women predominate—the sort of people George Belcher used to draw. They sit in the shadow of the great portly casks, exchanging grievances and making alternate trips to the bar, until the grievances grow less formidable, the world becomes less grey, and the prosperous days before they lost their husbands seem less far away.

Of course there are other patrons of the wine houses, such as designing-looking men out with girls who look so respectable that one wonders if they still cherish the old delusion that port wine is a temperance drink. But the Belcher types give them their character. If you want to see drink used as an escape from tribulation, to watch how to get just a shade tiddly without losing your self-respect, then you might do worse than go to an old-fashioned wine house in the neighbourhood of the Edgware Road.

THE WEST END

A VAGUE term in itself, 'the West End' is even vaguer when applied to pubs. Between Charing Cross and Hyde Park (to take fairly narrow limits for the West End) you can find everything from the big corner pub to the small quiet pub in the mews. There are houses where they sell nothing on draught except bitter and houses where there is a steady call for ale. Some of the humblest pubs are in the most expensive parts, such as the Punch Bowl in Farm Street and the Red Lion in Crown Court between King Street and Pall Mall. There are plenty of modernised pubs, but nothing more imposing than those that you see in all the suburbs from Barnet to Park Royal.

All you can say about the West End is that it has lots of pubs and plenty of variety amongst them, providing ample choice not only for regulars but for sightseers and theatre crowds. There is perhaps a slightly higher likelihood of getting food in the West End pubs than in those, say, of Lambeth and Battersea, and a larger proportion of pubs have restaurants attached, catering mostly for the lunch trade. There may be a rather higher proportion of pubs having no Public Bar, but when they do have one the prices in it are no higher than they are anywhere else.

The West End is, of course, more apt than some districts to suffer from the incursions of what we used to call the Bright Young People; what I now think of as the Flash Trade. This menace has receded since pre-war days when the smart people were discovering the pubs and the craze for darts even brought them swarming into the Public Bar. It was a terrible thing to see this happening to a pub. If it persisted, the old regulars abandoned the pub, the brewers redecorated it, the staff changed. At this stage the bright young people often deserted it for another, leaving a wreck behind. The worst of all these tragedies was that of the Running Horse in Shepherd Market, which I can remember when it was a decent, straightforward, plate-glass-and-mahogany back-street pub. This unfortunate house attracted the wrong sort of bright

The Private Bar at the Goat

people, and the end of it all was the extinction of the licence and disappearance of the sign.

That happened in 1936 and it is still an awful warning to the licensed trade. But the incursions of the more respectable flash are still going on. Shepherds in Shepherd Market, the elegant house where the telephone-box is disguised as a sedan chair, was built for them on the site of the New Chesterfield, and this was considerate of Carrs, for besides being quite a nice house when you are in the mood for that sort of thing, it draws off a lot of people who would otherwise get into the three other Market pubs. The Red Lion in Waverton Street has been turned inside out for them so that it is no longer the quiet resort that it used to be; and the last time I was in the Blue Posts off St. James's Street I saw symptoms that it might be going the same way.

But the curly moustaches, the scarlet fingernails, the Old School ties and the New Look blondes, are not only to be found in Mayfair and St. James's. There are pubs where they flourish in Bayswater and Bloomsbury and Marylebone and Chelsea; it was at the Antelope in Eaton Terrace that the staff used to call the Public Bar the Men's Bar, in contrast to the Saloon, and the pub where they label the Saloon the Sherry Bar is on Campden Hill. Whilst in none of these districts will you find a more modest exterior nor a cosier Private Bar than in the Goat off Old Bond Street, which Ardizzone has drawn.

EATING IN PUBS

IT IS impossible to avoid the touch of nostalgia when it comes to food. Before the war it could be claimed that London pubs provided as good food of its kind as you could get in England, and perhaps I may for one sad moment recall the cold sausages at the Nag's Head in Covent Garden, the steak-and-kidney pudding at the Windsor Castle dive in Victoria, the Saloon Bar lunch at the Peacock in Maiden Lane (joint and two veg, but the best of English meat and English cooking with all the gravy); the bread and cheese at Mooney's, the Welsh rarebits at the King Lud, the smoked salmon at the George in Wardour Street, the oysters at Ward's in Piccadilly Circus and De Hems. Even as late as the time of the flying-bombs, there was a steak pie at the Rose of Normandy that I cannot forget.

Food is a problem now for the pubs as for everybody else, but the machinery remains the same. You can still find everything varying from the separate restaurant to the dish of sandwiches on the bar. Many Saloon Bars give up a good deal of their counter space to food, especially at lunch time; many pubs have snack bars, which sometimes serve hot meals as well as cold; many have tables in the bar at which regular meals are served at midday. Such bars have their regular lunchers and it is not often that you see a chair empty between one o'clock and two.

The separate restaurant is a luxury that you find mainly in central London, though by no means only there. The licensing justices have long looked kindly on the separate restaurant as being less conducive to drink (though in fact many of the people who lunch regularly in the bar do not drink with their meals). There are imposing restaurants having little connection with the bars, like those at the Chandos in St. Martin's Lane, the Punch House off the Haymarket, the Garrick in Green Street, which looks more like a French café than most English restaurants, and the Horseshoe in Tottenham Court Road, which has succeeded in rivalling the old-world atmosphere of Fleet Street although I well remember when the house was built. There are smaller restaurants such as those at the White Horse in Newburgh Street, the Mason's Arms in Maddox Street, and the Spread Eagle in Oxford Street, which Ardizzone has drawn. These are more truly part of the pub but they are discreetly segregated from the bars, even if you approach them through the Public Bar, as you do at the Antelope, one of the few pub restaurants I know that is open for lunch and dinner on Sundays as well as during the week.

The great merit of the Snack Bars is that you can see your food before you order it and you can, if you wish, get through your meal in the minimum time. There are well-known snack bars at De Hems in Macclesfield Street, (where the stairs and restaurant are walled entirely in oyster-shells), at Shelley's in Stafford Street, the Punch Tavern in Fleet Street, amongst many more. But the longest snack bar in London must be the enormous one in the Dive at the Windsor Castle, outside Victoria Station, where they have also under the one roof an imposing restaurant, another Snack Bar in the Saloon, and a delicatessen where you can buy things to take away. More food must change hands, I should think, in the Windsor Castle than in any other pub in town.

As for the sandwiches that you buy over the bar, they are a gamble now wherever you go. Sometimes you strike lucky with beef or tongue; more often all London seems to be eating pink paste or old shoe-leather, and you sigh for honest bully-beef or genuine Spam. But that is a feeling not confined to the bar, and at least they have fewer fancy names for rubbish than they have in the restaurant upstairs.

Dining Room at

the Spread Eagle

THE RIVERSIDE PUB

THERE are as many different uses for the pub as a man can have moods. There is the hasty recourse for a quick one, or the occasion best exemplified by the 'arf a pint each that Ginger Dick and Peter Russett had at a public-'ouse at the top of the Minories, 'just to steady themselves' before they went to rob old Sam. There is the lunch-time visit, the refresher after a bout of work, the adjournment to celebrate something, the casual visit to see if you can find your friends, every variation down to the ignominious refuge from a shower of rain. But the most innocent and laudable of all occasions is probably the deliberate search of a long, quiet evening's drinking in pleasant surroundings, even in the open air.

For this purpose the riverside pub is justly famed. There is something soothing in the sluggish water and the slow tempo of river traffic that conduces to the leisurely enjoyment of drink. The motor-boats spoil it, of course, when they go scooting and puffing up and down, but at least there are no motor-cars. To sit on the balcony of a down-river pub at slack tide, watching a few rowing-boats thread their way among the moored barges, gives you the feeling of tranquillity that I imagine our fathers must have enjoyed when they sat in the shade outside a roadside pub in the country, and the slow transit of an occasional cart became an event to watch with fascination and celebrate at its conclusion with another drink.

The riverside pubs have become famous but they are largely unspoiled. There was a time when you could not go down Narrow Street or Wapping Wall on a fine evening without being assailed by piercing voices from the West End, but I think the age of going to pubs for excitement has passed, leaving the pubs unimpaired.

Like the tea-shops at Bushey Park, the riverside pubs fall into two categories, those that go through and those that don't; though unlike the tea-shops those that fall in the wrong category do not put up mirrors to delude the unwary into going in. There

The Balcony at the Angel

are some very nice old houses in riverside streets that do not look directly on to the river, but it is not worth while penetrating the deserted streets lined with towering warehouses unless you have the water itself to reward you at the end.

The Angel at Rotherhithe is not the most famous of these pubs; it has not the associations of the Town of Ramsgate by Wapping Old Stairs, where they caught Judge Jeffreys, or of the Grapes in Limehouse, which has been identified as the Six Jolly Fellowship Porters of 'Our Mutual Friend'. It is not even so popular a resort for sightseers as the Prospect of Whitby in Wapping Wall. But as Ardizzone's drawing will indicate, it is as pleasant a place as you could find for an evening drink, when the Pool is quiet and you can watch every stick of driftwood floating down to Shadwell from the Tower Bridge.

Of course the other end of London has its riverside pubs too, though fewer than you would expect. London has never used its riverfront to the best purpose, and this is one of the ways in which it has fallen short. There are famous pubs on the Boat Race course—the Doves at Chiswick is perhaps a shade too famous now, but there are other houses along the Mall and on the towing-path at Putney which have a river view from their windows even though you cannot drink with the water lapping under your feet; but how much a few more of them would improve the neglected South bank from Battersea down!

Perhaps this is one of the things the re-planners will get around to in time, and the rebuilding of the South side for the 1951 Festival will give them a good chance. A pleasance is a nice new idea, but there is a lot of experience in favour of the pub.

THE IRISH HOUSE

IT WILL not have escaped the perceptive reader that this book has its partialities. Ardizzone does not attempt to conceal his weakness for antique elegance in pub architecture and I have no desire to hide my own leaning to Guinness's stout on draught. Both these predilections meet in full flood at Mooney's in the Strand.

Guinness on draught has spread far beyond the Irish houses, as has been mentioned elsewhere in this book. And there are other Irish houses, indeed other Mooney's. But this one in the Strand always seems to me the father and mother of them all.

It owes something to geography, of course; amongst all the rebuilding, it and its neighbour Romano's survive to remind us of the days when the Strand was the centre of London's entertainment in a way that no London street is now. In my case it owes much to personal associations, for it was there that I used to drink with the uniformed staff of the BBC when the BBC was at Savoy Hill and its white-collared officials infested all the more pretentious of the local bars.

In those days it was partitioned off into two bars and a snug, distinguished by no difference in price or fare but lending themselves to the ritual of lunching in the snug and then having one for the road in each of the bars on the way out. Removal of the partitions has for once, I think, actually improved the house. You now get a clear view of the long lofty room, with the narrow pink marble bar typical of Mooney's running right down it, and faded allegorical paintings barely disclosing their unfashionable charms from the high walls. Apart from the paintings its furnishings are purely utilitarian, and the bar is graced by those imposing tall wooden casks that hold wine and spirits on draught. Unless you are a connoisseur of wine, you can get a feeling of old-fashioned grandeur by ordering a glass of port on draught and seeing the barman raise a pink head on the tall glass; and if you are a connoisseur of whiskey you might do worse than try a ball of malt direct from the wood.

70

Mooney's Bar

In happier days Mooney's was a wonderful place for value in food as well as drink. Their bread, butter, cheese, and pies were as genuine as the draught stout, and a pint of stout, bread, butter, and cheese, all for one-and-twopence, made a good start to anybody's lunch. The value extended to the drawing of the stout, and still does. No barmaid ever worked at Mooney's; their barmen come from Dublin, and they are all experts in the art of getting the correct creamy head on a well-filled pint.

The green clock of Mooney's hangs outside other good pubs besides the one in the Strand. There is, for instance, one in Oxford Street near Soho Square, one at Cambridge Circus, one in Fleet Street, one in Fetter Lane with a particularly friendly landlord, one in Holborn (besides the one that was bombed), one just over London Bridge. You can find City variants of the species in Coleman Street and St. Mary Axe. There is the rival firm of Ward's, who have Irish Houses all over the town: there is one in Bull's Head Alley off the Strand, one mercifully close to the Central Hall, Westminster, one at the corner of Gray's Inn Road, one disguised as the Sun and Horseshoe in Mortimer Street, but the pivot of them all is the one below Piccadilly Circus, with an entrance next to the London Pavilion, which can share with the theatre the claim to be placed at the Centre of the World.

This central Ward's is perhaps the most Irish of the Irish Houses in its fittings, but it has a cosmopolitan clientèle; overseas visitors find their way to it as soon as they arrive in London. It used to have a celebrated oyster bar, and it is still a good place to get a meal.

It takes all sorts to make a world, and I have taken many a horse to the water and found him too saucy to drink. But anybody who is interested in London pubs should not rest from searching until he has once leaned his elbows on the pink marble at Mooney's in the Strand.

GAMES

STANDARDS of behaviour in the pubs are very strict. You must not dance or sing or the landlord will start talking about his licence, you must not bet or pass betting slips, and you must not play even cribbage for money. All the same, pub-goers have at their command a most extensive range of games, and new ones are still coming in.

Let us dismiss the machine games, though it is true that to look round some Saloon Bars you might almost think you were on a pier. Pin-tables flash, ring, and rattle, and you may even find patrons unwise enough to torment themselves by trying to smack their pennies through a mimic golf course for the satisfaction of sometimes getting one back. But apart from the machines, the pubs can provide games of all kinds from the new-fangled bar billiards to the old-fashioned skittles, if you know where to go.

Real billiards and snooker are dying out in the pubs, though you still find the faded splendour of a billiard-room here and there (there is a typical one at the Phoenix behind Oxford Circus, a house that is in many ways redolent of the Edwardian past). The full-blooded form of skittles in which you hurl the cheese full pitch at the pins requires an alley that few pubs possess; the Black Lion at Chiswick, celebrated by A. P. Herbert, is the best known, but I have pleasant memories of the alley at the King's Head at Roehampton not so many years ago. Bowls is a rare luxury, and even the Six Bells and Bowling-Green in King's Road has ceased to live up to its name. Table skittles is found here and there, but I think the rings have entirely vanished from the London pubs. The immemorial games that survive are the games of the Public Bar: dominoes, shove-ha'penny, and darts.

Dominoes is a quiet, intellectual game, which I fancy is on the decline. Shove-ha'penny is a game of skill, which has become fashionable in the last ten years. Not so fashionable, however, as darts. The darts craze once threatened to change the very character of the pubs, but its worst dangers seem to have passed away.

Darts at the Alfred

Not that darts is any less popular than it was; it is played more than ever, and records and matches even get into the news. But it seems now to be played in the pubs by people who would go to the pubs anyway. The danger came when darts, from being a thoroughly plebeian game, jumped into fashion; when higher Civil Servants began carrying their own set of arrows about in their waistcoat pockets and young women who wanted to do what was being done pursued the darts-board into the Public Bar. For a time the long-established social stratification of the pubs was knocked sideways, and the chief victims were the regulars of the cheap side. However much they might resent the invasion they could not retaliate; they were not going to pay more in the Saloon.

Luckily help was at hand. Landlords who had at first welcomed the new custom saw their regulars disappearing and their Saloons standing empty whilst people who had previously drunk bottled Bass or Scotch-and-soda discovered the advantages of wallop at fivepence a pint. The cure was very simple: a darts-board in the Saloon. England being what it is, social distinctions soon re-asserted themselves, to the relief of both sides.

Darts is played more than ever: every night hundreds of thousands of people get healthy exercise following their arrows to the board, and perform miracles of mental arithmetic which they could never achieve with pencil and paper when faced by a Government form. But it is no longer a cult. As soon as you could play it wherever you liked—in the club, the canteen, the A.R.P. post, the Saloon Bar—it lost its appeal for the novelty-seekers and became again a game that you play if you enjoy it and not unless. And if it does sometimes interfere with serious drinking, in present conditions that is perhaps just as well.

DRUNKS

DRUNKENNESS, as has been previously mentioned, plays little part in the life of the pubs. This is not because of the difficulty of getting drunk on contemporary beer, for this difficulty can be solved by the resolute, but because drunkenness everywhere is going out, at least in its public manifestations, and it is particularly unpopular in the pubs, where the landlord fears for his licence and the other frequenters resent the interference with their own comfort that it is apt to cause.

The days of 'Drunk for a penny, dead drunk for twopence, clean straw for nothing' are far off in the dead past. In my own early days closing-time was apt to bring its incidents, though you rarely saw even the beginnings of a real stand-up fight; and now and again you came across a sad and bewildered character trying to make up his mind to leave the bar where he had been firmly refused any more. But such symptoms have been declining steadily and I cannot remember meeting a drunk in a pub since the war.

During the war, of course, things were different. It is one of the immemorial privileges of the military to get drunk when they can find the time, and now that they no longer wear bayonets it is not so dangerous to the public as it was once. And it is, I hope, not ungrateful to admit that our overseas allies often brought with them drinking habits rather more violent than ours.

It was unfortunate for the Londoner that he became exposed to the depredations of drunks, with which he had become unfamiliar, just when he was cutting down his own drinking in reaction from the first impact of the rise in price and shortage of supplies. When you are wondering whether you ought not to make it a half this time, it is galling to see somebody else ordering a double and a pint to chase it with, and I often speculate on the private life of that GI in the Dover Castle during the early spirits shortage, who kept on ordering rounds of four double rums and carrying them away to a corner of the bar until Mooney told him the rum was running short and asked him if his friends could not drink some-

The Drunk

thing else. 'What do you mean, friends?' he said. 'These are for me'. Much as one sympathises with anybody who finds the pub double a small dose, this was going a bit far.

Drunks are apt to be a nuisance, but there are drunks whom one remembers with kindness. There was one such whom I met years ago in the Peacock in Maiden Lane before it was rebuilt. He tried to get me to have one with him and to take his money and give the order, saying with an air of transparent cunning 'You see, I mightn't get served'. He told me how he had a fine house out at Ealing, 'but what's the good of it when I can't find it? I've been out there every day.' I helped him out at closing-time and he clung tightly to my arm, confiding pathetically 'You know I'm quite all right, but I've got these rubber things on my shoes, and they catch in things and then I fall down.' I often wondered whether he ever got back to his house. Looking at it impartially, I cannot see any strong likelihood that he ever would.

But drunks are not the only menace to the internal peace of the pubs. I remember once a stranger approached me in the Tivoli Bar and tried to get into conversation. Not feeling in the mood to talk to a stranger I rebuffed him rather harshly and he retired to his seat. The barmaid came up to me and leaned across the bar. 'I'm glad you ticked him off,' she whispered. 'I don't think he's quite right in the head. Do you know what that is he's reading? A religious book.'

MUSICIANS

Pub-goers have been hit in various ways by post-war economic factors, and perhaps this book has harped somewhat on the point. Let me now admit that we have had our compensations too. For instance, in this age of full employment, direction, and so on, mendicancy is at a discount, and this makes things much more peaceful in the pubs.

Pub-goers are notoriously generous; perhaps because the pub is a resort of comparative plenty, and everybody who goes in to buy himself a drink knows that he has at least that much money to spare and everybody will naturally assume that he has more. There is a good deal of pathos in the sight of somebody else who has come into the pub not to indulge himself but to beg from those who can. Unless you are literally down to the price of your last drink your hand goes to your pocket more readily than it would in the street; you feel at once generous and superior, and it in no way impairs those feelings if you have reason to think that when the mendicant has called at one or two more houses he will be able to become a customer himself at a third.

So into the pubs used to come a stream of men and women selling (or offering for sale) bootlaces, matches, collar-studs, books, and flowers. There was one genial merchant whose stock-in-trade varied from enormous silver watches to a portable try-your-weight machine, but I fancy he is still around. And the Salvation Army lasses still creep quietly into the pubs they would like to abolish, and do very well in donations in spite of their obvious conviction that they are daring all for the Cause by venturing among these evil men. (I must except the one who plies the pubs of the West End, is as well known in them as the brewer's man, and calls not only the staff but some of the most doubtful customers by their Christian names. Her sales of the *War Cry* must top all the rest.)

But the visitors I miss are the musicians, who, unlike the other mendicants, made a point of giving their performance first and

The Cornet Player

then coming round to solicit what was theoretically a thank-offering rather than alms.

One of the oldest sights in London was the performer on the tin whistle (usually made of brass, I believe, for by some technicality tin whistles were banned by law and brass whistles were not), with one foot inside the pub door, 'demonstrating for a penny the causes of his professional degradation'. But he was the lowest note in the musical scale. He did not expect you to enjoy his music; he was merely going through the motions of giving value for the money he hoped to receive, whereas the cornet, the accordion, most of all the multiple band were really giving value—whether you liked it or not.

At any moment a shake of the economic kaleidoscope may bring the musicians out again in their hordes, and test the genuineness of any regret that pub-goers may feel for them now that they are so rare. Personally I should prefer anything to the music that has taken their place. The wireless set usually plays away discordantly in the background until the landlord remembers it and impatiently turns it off, but the real horror is the juke-box. Even where the management has been so reckless as to install one, public opinion usually prevents its being used, but there is always the danger of the odd assertive individual like Kipps in the Royal Grand Hotel. Already more than one pub has been closed to me by a juke-box, and there is another where the monster crouches ready to be called into hideous life; the regulars have the sense to leave it alone, but any day a Frankenstein may walk in. The threat makes one almost long to hear again the plaintive piping of the tin whistle from just outside the door.

CAME THE BEER

BEFORE the war the arrival of the brewer's dray was merely a matter of routine. It was a picturesque incident; you had to be careful not to trip over ropes and fall head first down the open hatch, and at some pubs they had to close one door whilst the barrels came in. The landlord's children welcomed the diversion, but to the customer it didn't mean a thing.

There have been times since the war when the coming of the beer was an event rather like the sighting of the relief force from the walls of Lucknow. Kind men went and told their friends. There were even said to be syndicates of drinkers who employed men on bicycles to follow the drays through the streets and spread the glad tidings as soon as they stopped at a pub.

The beer famine varies with place and season; one day the publicans are complaining that they can't sell their beer, the next they are refusing pints, imposing shandy, even closing early and staying shut next day. The weather has a lot to do with it, of course, and it is particularly galling for the faithful drinker, who has struggled through the snowdrifts to drink freezing beer in an icy bar, when a few days later the sun comes out and he can't get served.

The worst of the famine, so far as my experience goes, was in the summer of 1946, when the boom was still on and too many people were chasing too little beer. My work then took me to the Northern heights, and I daily grieved to see the proportion of pubs closed on the well-furnished route from Portland Place to Muswell Hill. The Dive at Alexandra Palace, where the permitted evening opening is at 5.30, used to open at 7 for shandy and not until 8 for beer; and at lunch-time there would be a row of chalk-marks on the bar, and as each pint was served one mark would be expunged. When the last mark went you knew you would get no more beer.

In that remote spot the drying-up of the one pub was a real disaster. Otherwise, my experience was that you could always

The Beer arriving

find beer if you had long enough to look for it. Even at the worst of the drought, if you went on walking you came to an oasis, but very often it was a race with time.

I remember one warm evening when I set out for a pint and a snack. The Woodman was open and I had abandoned my transport before I discovered that bottled cocktails were all they had to sell. I walked the length of Archway Road and well into Holloway with no reward beyond a solitary half-pint, and the further I went the worse things got. When every pub I came to had a chalked notice saying 'Open 8 p.m.' I gave it up; but on the way back a faint indomitable flicker of hope made me turn aside to the Green Man on Muswell Hill, and there they were selling pints without stint.

The landlords might have co-operated more in those difficult days; too often all the pubs in a neighbourhood seemed to be closed on the same day. But they had their problems, as we pub-goers were ready to admit. I can quite believe that the good landlord, the sort who likes his customers and enjoys pulling a thirsty man a pint, must have felt very melancholy as he lurked in his upstairs living-room and peeped through the curtains at his regulars padding wearily away from the closed doors.

It made us more adventurous, it is true. In times of plenty it is easy to get into a rut about your pubs. One pub that you know to be good will blind you to others in the vicinity until one day you find the good pub closed. There is nothing like a barred door with 'Tuesday 7' chalked on it for sending you exploring again, and when you go into the highways and byways you are apt to be easily pleased with what you find. The house looks brighter, the landlord kinder, the beer tastes better, when it comes just as your legs are beginning to get tired.

OBITUARY

For those of us who feel sad whenever a pub vanishes, this is a sad life. Progress, reconstruction, town-planning, war, all have one thing in common: the pubs go down before them like poppies under the scythe.

The first pub that I remember mourning was the Man in the Moon that gave its name to a passage behind the old Quadrant in Regent Street—a very convenient spot. So far as I recollect it went even before the rebuilding of the Quadrant; a warehouse took it over, and I often wondered what happened to the pewter tankards that they had used as drip-cans under the taps. The Golden Cross, successor to the great coaching inn, went when they built South Africa House, and lessened by one the ordeals of that epic pub-crawl from Ludgate Circus to Trafalgar Square that we have all talked about and never done. I grieved particularly for the White Hart in Lexington Street, for it was a little quiet neglected house, with the door swinging on a strap and a step down to the bar, where I always felt that Bill Sikes might at any moment spring up from the deal tables with his white dog at his heels. And the passing of the Two Chairmen in Wardour Street meant that if you fancied Benskin's you had to go to far-flung houses like the Halfway House at Camden Town, the Holly Bush at Hampstead, the Flora Hotel in Harrow Road, or the Antelope beyond Eaton Square.

It is a sad thing to come across houses that have obviously been pubs and are so no more, like the Three Tuns in Clare Market, now a Students' Union, or the house in Marylebone Lane that looked so normal that I went into it before I found it was a policemen's club. I will not harp again on some of the painful casualties that have been mentioned elsewhere in these pages, but it is pleasant to recall one pub that went out in a blaze of glory: the Turk's Head at Wapping, near Execution Stairs, where the final advent of closing time was the occasion of the noisiest broadcast the BBC ever put out.

The Bombed Pub

The war of course made terrible inroads; the Luftwaffe worked faster than the brewers and the Bench. Pub-goers will not need Ardizzone's drawing to remind them of the pang caused by seeing a resort where you might have been drinking a few hours before, with its insides blown out and all the mysteries of Private and Public exposed to the passing gaze. The list of losses is too long to recite, but amongst those that I myself missed most were the Old Pitt's Head behind Hertford Street; the Devonshire in Hallam Street, one of the BBC's locals; the Royal Pair, a charming little pub in Clareville Grove off Gloucester Road; the Admiral Duncan in Old Compton Street, where vanloads of police were once called to quell a riot in the days of the race-gangs; and the Canterbury Arms in Lambeth Marsh, a nice bright little house near the side door of the famous music-hall that it had survived. And it was hard not to feel sorry for those complex and up-to-the-minute institutions, the Leicester Corner in Leicester Square and the Bedford Corner in Tottenham Court Road.

Happily, things were often not so bad as they first seemed. Many a pub that one had written off put out new shoots, and almost every pub that still has four walls standing is now in business again. Nothing looked more desolate, in the autumn of 1940, than the corner of Oxford Street and Tottenham Court Road, but today the Horseshoe shows no scars and even the Blue Posts is still working, with only one storey and two-thirds of a bar. There is a respectful pleasure in drinking at a house like this, or the Bunch of Grapes behind Selfridge's, where the ground floor alone survived a V2. And there are enough brewers' signs standing on razed sites to encourage the hope that some of these phoenixes will yet rise again.

AFTER HOURS

'LAST orders gentlemen please!' 'Time gentlemen please!' 'Drink up gentlemen please!' 'Past time gentlemen *please!*' With this nightly ritual does the law descend on the pubs, always unwelcome, and positively intolerable on Saturday nights.

The ritual, it must be admitted, is not always invoked. Nowadays the law is not the only thing that can close the pubs; lack of beer may do the same thing, and at unpredictable hours. The legal closing time has come to mean less to landlords and the customer has lost heart about his rights. In big pubs, such as the Windsor Castle, they might lower the lights and ring the bells as early as 10.50 p.m. on Saturdays, knowing that it would take them a full ten minutes to clear the bar, but this happened every Saturday. It did not take you by surprise. Now, you may look in at 10.30 and find the cloths draped over the beer-pulls; or you may take your glasses back to the bar and be told that they have stopped serving or that there is no more beer. What you can't have you want, but there is no warning. You can no longer sit over half-a-pint all the evening and then spring to your feet and fight your way to the bar when the cry of 'Last orders' rends the air.

Still, some pubs do sometimes last out until the legal closing-time, and it is then that you come across those sad little groups such as Ardizzone has drawn. These are not the people who rush out of the pubs to be sick into the gutter, for addicts of this regrettable and diminishing habit can seldom wait until closing time, and when they recover they stagger hurriedly away. Nor are they those who cause crowds to collect by giving illusory promise of a fight (and it is seldom now that you see even the promise of a fight either inside or outside a London pub). These are the people who use the pubs; who meet their friends there, talk there, exchange the news there, and prefer the cheerful company of the bar to the strait confines of their home. They cannot bear to say goodbye to all that. They linger on the pavement, carrying on the conversations they have begun in the warm

94

After Hours

bright bar, whilst the lights go out behind them, the bolts are shot noisily home, and the iron gates close with a clang.

It is surprising how long they linger there. Half-an-hour after closing time, sometimes, you can still see them, little knots from which every now and then a reluctant unit detaches itself and slinks solitary home.

On Saturday night they linger longest. On that night the bar is warmest, the greatest proportion of the population has met in it, and the gap before it opens again is widest. If the pubs did open earlier on Sunday few of these people would be up in time to go to them, for the long lie on Sunday is the Londoner's great luxury of the week; but at closing-time on Saturday night, opening-time on Sunday seems an age away.

The exceptions to the curfew are fewer than they used to be, too. Supper extensions have vanished, so you can't drink until midnight in a pub even if you are willing to pay for a token sandwich with every drink. The shrinkage has affected home supplies; you can rarely hope to take a couple of quarts home with you or to find beer waiting for you at home; and both proceedings are still regarded with some disfavour by many wives who have no scruple about accompanying their husbands to the pub.

The one person still privileged is the landlord, who may be glad enough to get to bed on a Saturday night but who knows that there is nothing to prevent his coming down and having what he likes in the empty bar on Sunday, long before the doors are opened to admit the faithful who are already waiting hopefully outside.

GLOSSARY OF TERMS
COMMONLY USED IN CONNECTION
WITH THE LONDON PUBS

ALE. In London pubs ale stands for mild ale, which is the mildest, weakest, and cheapest sort of draught beer. It is reddish-brown in colour, not unlike Burton to look at, but of lower specific gravity. In the Public Bar pints of ale are the staple drink; in fact if you go into the Public Bar and ask for a pint, without specifying the brew, you get ale, just as in the Saloon Bar you would get bitter. Mild ale is often drunk mixed with bitter (mild-and-bitter) or Burton (old-and-mild). It can also be mixed with strong ale or stout.

The rise in the price of beer has caused the habit of drinking mild ale to spread to the Saloon, where it used not to be welcomed by landlords, who regarded it as rather too cheap a drink for that select side, and sometimes did not even serve it there. On the other hand it quite often happens that you find a house is out of bitter and has nothing to serve but mild. Some breweries make more than one quality of mild, and if you like a sweetish beer you will find these special milds extremely good.

Light Mild (not to be confused with *Light Ale*, q.v.) is a mild ale lighter in colour than the ordinary mild: more the colour of bitter. This is not often met with in London pubs. (See also *Brown Ale*, *I.P.A.*, *Light Ale*, *Pale Ale*, *Scotch Ale*, *Strong Ale*, *Winter Ale*.)

Note: the preference of literary men for the term 'ale', as being more romantic than 'beer', has caused many misunderstandings. Foreigners for instance, reading of 'a tankard of ale in a tavern' (instead of 'a pint of beer in a pub') sometimes ask for ale in London pubs, get ale, and think that English beer is even weaker than it is. Incidentally, ale is not usually drunk from tankards in London, as it is chiefly a Public Bar drink, and tankards are seldom seen in the Public Bar.

Note 2: although it has really nothing to do with this book, piety compels me to acknowledge that my own home drink for many years has been Fremlin's Family Ale, which I chose originally merely on the grounds of cheapness, and which I have found makes an ideal steady drink for all times of day. This is a light mild on draught such as you seldom see in pubs.

BAR. Usually, a place where drink is sold over the counter for consumption on the premises (but see *Bottle-and-Jug*). The standard equipment for a London pub is three bars—Public, Private, and Saloon—but there are many variations, such as Ladies' Bar, Lunch, Buffet, Snack, and Wine Bars, apart from Lounges and Dives (q.v.). The term 'bar' is also used for many places that are not regular pubs, though they may sell draught beer (e.g. the Tivoli Bar in the Strand and the Craven Bar in Craven Street). A number of these not-quite-pubs are referred to in this book, the line of demarcation being very arbitrary, so long as they sell draught beer.

Note: by Lady Astor's Act of 1923, a bar became known to the legislature as a place where a person under eighteen years of age may not have a drink, though in a restaurant (if he can afford to go to licensed restaurants) he can have what he likes.

BAR PARLOUR. Formerly, a select apartment behind the bar where regular customers foregathered. Now rarely encountered in London pubs.

BARLEY WINE. Extra strong beer, either in bottle or on draught. The best-known probably is Bass's barley wine, which used to be sold on draught as well as in bottle at a number of houses in the West End, and cost as much before the war as quite ordinary bitter does now. It is really a sort of liqueur beer. (See also *Number 1, Strong Ale.*)

B-B. An abbreviation for bitter and Burton mixed half-and-half.

BEER. A generic term for all malt liquors; it is sometimes used to include even stout. If you ask for 'beer' in a London pub without specifying what beer you want, you will probably get bitter—if they have got it.

BEER-ENGINE. The machine by which draught beer, stout etc. is pumped up from the cellars to the taps in the bar. The handling of the beer-engine can make a considerable difference to the taste of the beer, and its state of cleanliness can make even more. In recent years a great many improvements have been made in the direction of keeping the beer at an even temperature and keeping the pipes between the cellar and the bar clean. Some types of beer-engine have the glass pipes visible through or over the bar-counter, so that you can see your beer coming up.

BEERHOUSE. A house licensed to sell ales and beers, and sometimes wines, but not spirits. There are not many of these in central London, though I know of one or two, but the proportion is higher in some outlying parts; for instance, I have come across three in a row in New Cross. During the spirits shortage after the war a number of licensees began to talk bitterly about the unrewarding expense of a spirits licence and say they might as well keep a beerhouse and save their money, but I have seen no signs of their doing it yet.

BEER-PULLS. The handles of the beer-engine. In older pubs the long row of china beer-pulls, usually mounted on brass, is the chief distinguishing feature of any bar. Modern pubs, with fewer varieties of drink on draught and devices for changing the cask that serves any one pump, have fewer beer-pulls; sometimes they even use taps under the bar instead. For a long time china beer-pulls were regarded as old-fashioned and newly-fitted pubs had them of black wood or sometimes of chromium. Now the movement seems to be towards keeping the china when they are lucky enough to have it.

BINDER. A final drink, usually a short one after a series of beers. The progression of drinks for two drinkers might be described as follows: 'Have one with me', 'the other half', 'the odd', 'a final', 'a binder', 'one for the road'.

BITTER. A clear beer of a golden colour with a strong element of hops, which is the staple draught drink in the Saloon Bar. Can be mixed with mild ale, Burton, or stout.

Note: connoisseurs of bitter have their various fancies but there is a good deal of agreement on Bass's bitter, especially when it is drawn from the wood. Bass on draught is to be found in Wenlock houses and in a large number of other pubs, most of which advertise the fact by a sign. Worthington is another much-favoured bitter. Rare brews for London which have their supporters are Benskin's (Antelope, Halfway House, Holly Bush, Flora Hotel), Simonds's (Devereux), and Shepherd Neame (Rutland, West Smithfield).

BLACK VELVET. A drink made by mixing champagne and stout, noted as an excellent pick-me-up; very expensive but once fashionable though rather fast. An attempt was made before the war to popularise it and some pubs put up a printed notice advertising it and quoting a price, but I have not seen or heard of it as a pub drink since the war.

BOTTLE-AND-JUG BAR. A bar reserved for people buying drinks to take away. Selling drinks for consumption at home used to be quite an important branch of the trade, particularly around closing time, but few pubs nowadays have a special bottle-and-jug bar and there is no legal obstacle to buying and selling beer to take away over the bar. There is however at present a very practical obstacle. Bottles are in even shorter supply than beer. They have always been a valuable property, with threepence allowed on the quart bottle, but after the war they became so hard to get that a newcomer to a neighbourhood who had not brought his bottles with him had great difficulty in getting any beer to take home. The matter was even raised in the correspondence columns of *The Times*, and the solution finally proposed was to raid the nearest rubbish-dump.

As an alternative to buying bottled beer, some people have always brought their own jugs or bottles (hence the name of the bar) and had them filled from the taps, thus obtaining the advantages of draught beer in the home. This practice has also been gravely affected by the shortage of beer; if the landlord knows that his self-allotted quota will run out before closing time, he does not like to let other customers see anybody taking any quantity away. (See pp. 42-45; also *Off-Licence*.)

BROWN ALE or BROWN BEER. A bottled beer corresponding more nearly to Burton than to bitter. Occasionally used for Burton on draught.

BUFFET BAR. In pubs this may mean a snack bar, or it may be only a grandiose term for a Saloon Lounge or Saloon Bar.

BURTON. A draught beer darker and sweeter than bitter, named originally after the great brewing town of Burton-on-Trent but now common to all breweries wherever they are. Burton is also known as 'old'. Popular compounds are B-B (bitter and Burton) and old-and-mild (mild and Burton). Some pubs used to keep a special Burton which was more of a strong ale and made an excellent mixture with mild, having more body than the ordinary Burton even when mixed. Many pubs do not keep Burton during the hot weather, counting it a winter drink, and since the war some breweries have reduced the season still further; one landlord told me he had had two barrels at Christmas and no more all the year. (See *Old*.)

CAN. A name for a tankard, used mostly in the Saloon Bar. 'Half-a-can' means half-a-pint of bitter in a tankard.

CANNED BEER, well known in America, has never caught on in London to any great extent. Beer was canned in England (or I believe it was Wales) before the war and some people ordered it from grocers, but it plays no part in the pubs. It may of course yet have a come-back as an item of Marshall Aid.

CHAMPAGNE used to be the hall-mark of flash aspirations in a pub. Quite a number of Saloon bars were willing to serve champagne cocktails if you ordered enough to make it worth while opening whatever was the smallest sized bottle they had, and some displayed conspicuously a permanent bottle of champagne ready to be served on draught; for that purpose it was mounted head downwards and secured by a powerful spring.

CHASER. A long drink drunk as a complement to a short drink. The name is American but the habit is well known in the British Isles. In Ireland whiskey is chased with water, in Scotland whisky is often chased with beer, and English sailors frequently drink rum and Burton alternately, this being a very intoxicating mixture.

CIDER. Most London pubs keep bottled cider and some have cider on draught, especially in the summer or when beer is short. Most often it is sweet cider rather than rough. Henekeys specialise in draught cider; they used to serve it in blue mugs at sixpence a pint, at which price it was very good value, being much stronger than it appeared at the time. The Constitution in Pimlico, which is a Henekey house, serves it from beer-engines and does a large trade in the Public Bar. Many pubs keep a keg of draught cider, and some are still known as Cider or Cyder Houses. Among these, Shattock's at the beginning of the Harrow Road, and the Cyder Stores near St. George's Circus are still genuine resorts of cider-drinkers, and both have an atmosphere quite unlike that of most pubs.

CLOSING TIME. The legal time at which pubs are compelled to close. This time, like the legal opening time, varies bewilderingly between different districts, and people who live near frontiers can profit from the fact; for instance, you can start your drinking at the Antelope before the Westminster pubs open and finish it down the road at the Duke of Wellington after the Chelsea pubs close. In Westminster (which stretches roughly from Oxford Street to the river and from Knightsbridge to Aldwych) the legal hours are: Weekdays, 11.30 a.m. to 3 p.m. and 5.30 p.m. to 11 p.m.; Sundays, 12.30 p.m. to

2.30 p.m. and 7 p.m. to 10 p.m. Some other London neighbourhoods open and close earlier. 12 p.m. is a common Sunday opening time outside Westminster, but I do not know of any district where the Sunday evening time is earlier than 7 p.m. No pubs stay open after 11 p.m. for drink alone, though there are *Extensions* (q.v.). Certain pubs in the neighbourhood of the markets open in the early morning for the convenience of market workers, but they are not supposed to serve drinks to anybody else.

Note: to make sure that their customers are not taken unawares by closing time and deprived of their penultimate drink, the pubs have a long-standing habit of keeping their clocks fast. You can usually count on having five or ten minutes in hand of whatever the pub clock says, and it has become an axiom amongst pub-goers that Pub Clocks Are Always Fast. Here and there however you find a pub that keeps its clock at the right time, thus fooling everybody but the regulars.

Note 2: the legal times of opening and closing, which used to be all-important, are now often obscured by the practical times, which depend on supplies and are quite variable. Legally pubs can be compelled to start serving at the official time but since the war this has not been enforced. They are however compelled to stop at the legal time even if they still have drink to sell. (See pp. 94-97.)

COCKTAILS. These are not popular in London pubs and when sold at all they are frequently poured direct from a bottle, which is all that people who want cocktails in pubs really deserve.

COCKTAIL BARS. Some of these qualify for consideration here by keeping draught beer—often a keg of Flowers. They very seldom, however, have facilities for keeping it well.

COLD DOG. Sometimes used for cold sausages, which have always been a popular comestible in the pubs. Unlike 'hot dog', it does not imply a roll.

COLLAR. A name for the gap between the top of the beer and the top of the glass, which has become increasingly important with the rise in the price of beer; on the whole, the higher the price the less you seem to get in the glass.

Note: this question of measure is quite a problem, as the measures stamped and passed by the excise people contain the exact legal pint or half-pint when they are filled to the brim. There is no allowance for froth or spilling. In happier days landlords and barmaids usually filled the measure at the cost of letting some beer run over, though most restaurants made plenty of allowance for spilling and did not like it if you sent the can back to be filled up. Nowadays most pub-goers' experience is that you very often get pints and half-pints with a handsome collar between the head and the rim, and it is seldom indeed that you have a chance to blow off the froth before you drink. At present prices, a collar of this kind may cost you a penny or two every time.

Bottled beers are not sold by measure so the bottle glass is not a legal measure and leaves plenty of room for the froth. Draught lager is often served in outsize glasses, some of which have an etched mark below the rim to show where the drink should come, regardless of froth. One pub serves draught Guinness in over-size glasses that hold a half-pint with the head, but as this sensible practice may be illegal I will avoid naming the pub.

CRIBBAGE. The traditional card game of the pubs, said to be the only one legally allowed there. Still played sometimes, usually in the Public Bar.

CRISPS. Cold chipped potatoes, sold in a paper bag with a screw of salt in a blue paper hidden amongst the crisps; very popular in the pubs but now of course in short supply.

CROWN TOP. The sort of metal cap, opened by leverage and not by screwing, that is now normally used for half-pint bottles. If by any chance you persuade a pub to sell you some bottles to take away and they are crown-tops, make sure you have an opener; it is a tantalising business doing it without.

DARTS. This game, indigenous to the pubs, had a remarkable boom during the few years before the war, and spread to all classes and to all the bars, as well as to living-rooms, clubs, and canteens. (Some of the effects of this boom are mentioned on pp. 38, 74-77.) The cult, fashion, or fad now seems to be over but the game is still more popular than it was ten years ago and is played habitually in the pubs, mostly in the Public Bar.

DIVE. A downstairs parlour or bar, usually specialising in food (oysters have a traditional association with dives). There are dives of every type, from the little snug at the Coal Hole in the Strand to the enormous café-bar at the Windsor Castle in Victoria, and they have little in common except that they do not charge less than Saloon prices. Some dives do not serve draught beer, so it is always wiser to enquire.

DOCK GLASS. A narrow but capacious wine-glass, much used in pubs and wine-houses.

DOG'S NOSE. A name for a rather insidious drink composed of beer with a drop of gin.

DOUBLE. A double whisky (Scotch implied unless you specify anything else); also known as a 'large whisky'. In this connection the term 'large' is purely comparative, as a double whisky in ordinary pubs is about one-sixteenth of a bottle and that is not very large. (See *Single*.) Since the war pubs have often refused to serve doubles when spirits were very short.

DOUBLE BROWN, DOUBLE BURTON, DOUBLE STOUT, etc. Names for special brews, but not by any means always to be taken literally.

DRAUGHT beer, stout, cider, or wine is served from the cask with or without the interposition of an engine, but without being bottled first. Draught beer is the characteristic drink of the London pubs, and in my own opinion far better than bottled beer, as it is usually cheaper and it is not gassy, as bottled beer often is. It is also the drink that varies most from brewery to brewery and from pub to pub, and therefore the one that needs most study by the pub-goer.

The drinks kept on draught in the ordinary London pub are bitter, Burton, and mild ale (the mild may be kept only in the Public Bar). To these may be added stout, a special bitter, special Burton, special ale, strong ale or barley wine, lager, cider, spirits, or wine. Most of these are dealt with under separate headings.

DROP. A single (whisky, gin, or rum); and a very expressive name for it too.

DRUNKENNESS is not now habitually encountered in London pubs, and the licensee is usually very much opposed to it, as it gives his house a bad name and may even jeopardise his licence. He will therefore probably refuse to serve a customer who seems to have had enough, and he is legally entitled to do this. He may, however, allow a regular customer to exceed a bit if he knows he is not likely to be troublesome, and especially if he is with friends. (See pp. 78-81.)

EXTENSION. A licence to open outside the usual licensing hours. Before the war many London pubs had a regular extension enabling them to stay open until midnight instead of closing at eleven o'clock, on condition that they did not sell drink without food. These houses used to close the bar-counter formally at eleven o'clock, and this accounts for the curious metal cages and sliding grilles that you see over some bars. There are also occasional extensions for sporting and public events and festivities such as a Coronation, and it is possible to get extensions for private parties, if it is worth the landlord's while to pay the fee.

Note: the two jokes about late-night or supper extensions were the property sandwich that you ordered so as to qualify for your drink and did not eat, so that it could be used over and over again until the edges began to curl; and the indignation of people who did not know the game, and were asked to pay a shilling for a sandwich when all they wanted was another drink.

Note 2: the best example of a permanent-occasional extension is the Tavern at Lord's, where they are allowed to serve drinks whenever cricket is being played. The prevailing shortage has done much to ruin this institution, but it used to be a feature not only of Lord's but of St. John's Wood. There was a whole breed of ardent drinkers who went to Lord's chiefly for the sake of being able to drink all the afternoon, and the old hands acquired an art of following the game without ever turning their backs to the bar.

FOUR-ALE BAR. The Public Bar. The old-fashioned term 'four-ale' is still used occasionally for mild ale. 'Six ale' for the better quality is sometimes used in the country, but I have not heard it in London.

FREE HOUSE. A pub not owned or controlled by any one brewer, and therefore free to draw its supplies from more than one source. (Opposed to *Tied House*, q.v.). Free houses are becoming increasingly rare, and most of those now surviving are owned by catering concerns that can compete with the breweries at the game of buying up pubs. Free houses owned by the landlord himself are now very few. Although the free house has been in process of being squeezed out for years, the claim is thought to have an appeal to pub-goers, and many pubs still bear it on their fascia-board although you may find only one brewer's products inside.

GILL. In wine and spirit measure, a quarter of a pint. 'Six out', meaning six out of a gill, gives you 32 tots to the bottle of whisky. The word is sometimes used loosely for a *half*-pint of beer, but this is largely a

Scottish custom and has never become naturalised in the London pubs. (See *Quartern*.)

GIN is fairly popular in pubs, where it is drunk with tonic, soda, water, lime-juice, or orange-juice; the traditional gin-and-peppermint is not often drunk now. A gin in beer is known as Dog's Nose but this again is no longer a common drink. Gin flavoured with Angostura bitters and filled up with water or soda is known as Pink Gin and is highly prized as a pick-me-up. Gin with Italian vermouth is known as Gin-and-It. The useful fluid can also be drunk with French vermouth, with mixed vermouth, or neat. The gin itself is usually London gin, not Plymouth or Hollands, but in the days of short supplies any kind of gin has a ready sale. Gin however has never been so rare as Scotch, which has a greater export value, and many drinkers have had to change their habits (see *Rum*).

GINGER ALE is often drunk with whisky (when there was rye it was of course part of the useful team of rye-and-dry), with gin (gin-and-ginger), and by itself as a teetotal drink (dry ginger). Amongst minerals it is rather more classy than, say, ginger-beer, which exists in the pubs mainly for its use in making *Shandy* (q.v.).

GINGER WINE is kept in some pubs and is a very warm and comforting drink. Taken with whisky it makes an excellent cold-weather cordial.

GLASS. 'A glass of beer' usually means half-a-pint, as opposed to a pint, even though most London pubs now serve everything in glasses from a drop of Scotch to a pint of ale. *Pewter* (q.v.) is generally considered to enhance the flavour of draught beer, but glass is certainly better for draught stout. Mooney's, for instance, where the draught Guinness is perfectly kept and professionally served, always use glass pots. Some barmaids do not know this and think they are treating you handsomely by drawing your draught stout in pewter tankards in the Saloon. For some reason bottled stout seems to go better in pewter than draught, and 'a couple of Guinness in a tankard' is a handy drink in restaurants and hotels where they have no draught beer.

Note: the change in fashions is well indicated by the remark made by one of W. W. Jacobs's characters that the Saloon Bar is a place where you get a penn'orth of beer in a glass and pay twopence for it. Glass and pewter have changed places since then. Glass is now almost universal in the Public Bar, even for pints, and the metal tankards are reserved for the Saloon. Glass however has a drawback in being a very formidable weapon. In the days of the race-gangs the first sign of trouble was often the smashing of a glass or bottle on the bar, the next move being to grind the splintered edges into somebody's face. Glasses and bottles are also dangerous when thrown. Pewter can of course also be used offensively, and in fact most old pub tankards have dents suggesting that they have at some time been bent over somebody's head; but it is not so wicked a weapon as broken glass.

Note 2: another drawback of post-war glass is that it is apt to disintegrate, owing, I believe, to its not being properly annealed. I have even known a beer-glass to explode, but this was in Broadcasting House and not in a regular pub.

GRANNY. A facetious term for old-and-mild, used in the East End and the docks. (Compare *Mother-in-Law*.)

GUT-ROT and Stomach-Wash. Facetious terms for ale.

HALF-AND-HALF. The old name for ale and porter mixed. It is not now used in this sense, but if you are ordering any mixture not altogether usual it does no harm to add 'half-and-half'.

HALF-PINT. The ordinary modest glass of beer, holding one-sixteenth of a gallon—the most frequent measure for the Saloon Bar. The 'pint' is usually omitted when ordering, as in 'half bitter please'. A small bottle of beer holds roughly half a pint.

HEAD. The froth on top of the beer. A good head is a traditional symptom of good beer well drawn, but for some years now it has ceased to be a reliable guide; you sometimes find brews in which the head seems to have little connection with the beer and you begin to suspect that the brewers' chemists could get a head on water if they tried. Still, there is a lot of appeal about the head on a good pint of bitter, sparkling like snow, or the rich smooth creamy head crowning a jet-black pint of stout.

HOPS are the element that makes beer bitter, and they have become a symbol for beer. I believe that the march of science has brought with it hop substitutes, but the big breweries maintain enormous hop-gardens in Kent.

ICE is not much used in English pubs unless they have a cocktail trade. It is still rather a luxury, reserved for very hot weather, when bottles of lager and light ale are placed in a bowl of ice on the bar. Some pubs also cool their draught beer in hot weather by packing ice round the pipes, but this should not normally be necessary if the cellars are properly cooled and there is enough custom to stop the beer from staying long in the pipes.

Note: this question of icing beer creates a gulf between fanciers of English beer and most visitors to the country. English beer is best enjoyed when it is only slightly below room temperature, but Americans and Europeans from lager-drinking countries marvel at the habit of drinking beer warm. Similarly, the beer-drinker from England suffers terribly when travelling in countries where the beer is habitually iced (i.e. all countries outside the British Isles) and has to be drunk in sips. Some of these iced beers would be undrinkable if they were not too cold to taste, but it is very sad if imported bottled beer is served too cold. In such cases you might try getting the barman to take your bottle off the ice and stand it in hot water before serving, just to take the chill off. This gives Americans a good laugh at the spectacle of the Englishman boiling his beer, but it is worth doing, especially with bottled Guinness, which loses all its flavour when iced.

INDIA PALE ALE (I.P.A.). A name for *Pale Ale* (q.v.), derived from the fact that bottled beer exported to India was the first to have its sediment removed, the reason being that it would otherwise ferment when in a tropical climate. It is now becoming obsolete even as a traditional name for a brew.

IRISH HOUSE. When a London pub calls itself an Irish House it usually means that it keeps Guinness on draught. Also you are sure of getting Irish whiskey, notably John Jameson, sometimes drawn from the wood. The best-known Irish Houses are the various Mooney's and Ward's. (See pp. 70-73.) Some of them are genuine resorts of the Irish in London, and particularly animated on such occasions as the Rugby International, the Grand National, and St. Patrick's Day.

IRISH WHISKEY is not very popular with London pub-goers, who tend to regard it as an inferior substitute for Scotch and drink it, when they have to, with soda, which is a great mistake. It can be drunk with water but the flavour is best obtained by drinking it neat with the water afterwards as a *chaser* (q.v.).

JUG-AND-BOTTLE BAR. (See *Bottle-and-Jug*, also pp. 42-45.)

LADIES' BAR. This is a relic of older manners, fast dying out. In pubs that have a Ladies' Bar only ladies are usually allowed in this bar, and ladies unaccompanied by a gentleman are not supposed to use the other bars. The Ladies' Bar belongs to the era of Phil May and George Belcher, and no rebuilt pub is likely to have one.

Note: quite a number of pubs exhibit a sign saying 'Ladies unaccompanied by a gentleman are not served in this bar', but these are usually in neighbourhoods where the ladies might be expected to visit the pub for the sake of Winning Friends and Influencing People rather than merely to have a drink. Ward's Irish House in Piccadilly Circus had such a sign but early in the war it went further and declined to serve ladies at all, though this monasticism did not last. In general, women are treated just like anybody else in the pubs.

LAGER is not a very popular drink in pubs, except in fairly high-class Saloon Bars during very hot weather. One can usually get bottled lager (especially in houses owned by Barclays, who brew an English lager) but it is not always iced. A few houses keep it on draught.

Note: The Prince's Head in Buckingham Street, off the Strand, used to keep lager in summer and stout in winter, and draw the stout through the lager pump. The result was amazingly good draught stout, but I have never encountered the method elsewhere.

LANDLORD. This name is still in use for the licensee of a pub, although he is now usually no more than a nominee of the brewery or even a salaried manager. The diminution in the real power of the 'landlord' is one reason for the dwindling of individual character in pubs, though it is only fair to say that the publican who is his own landlord can make a house intolerable too.

Note: some landlords and landladies have enough personality to become celebrities amongst pub-goers, but the days when celebrities took pubs seem to be going out. Since Tom Cribb's time it has been traditional for champion boxers to retire to pubs, and before 1939 they were still doing so: Ted Kid Lewis once had a house at Islington, Bombardier Billy Wells kept the original Mayfair Hotel in Down Street, George Cook once had the Devonshire Arms in Marylebone, and Jack Bloomfield the Sportsman's Saloon in Bear Street, Leicester Square; until the house was totally destroyed by bombing he was usually to be found behind the bar. George Mozart, the music-hall star, once kept the Green Man and French Horn in St. Martin's Lane, and there are various pubs kept by well-known footballers. One of the few recent instances of a celebrity going into the licensed victualling business that I have come across was when Rex Palmer, the original Golden Voice of the BBC, took the historic Dulwich Wood House in 1948.

LICENCE. The licence to sell beers and/or wines and spirits for consumption on the premises is one of the most highly prized of legal properties. There is an awful lot of law about it, and test cases affecting the rights and duties of inn-keepers and publicans occur periodically, as it is a very serious matter for a house to lose its licence. Nowadays most houses are owned by big firms of brewers or victuallers who employ the best of lawyers when licences are concerned. The effect of post-war shortages has been to remove from licensees the obligation that the pub-goer found most valuable —to keep open throughout licensing hours. (See under *Closing Time*.)

LICENSING LAWS. The elaborate system of legal obligations which determines what, when, and whom the licensee can serve without losing his licence. Few pub-goers know much about these laws except for those relating to closing-time and the ban on serving persons under 18, but I believe that the licensee is also entitled to refuse to serve any customer, drunk or sober, stranger or regular, in the Saloon or Private Bars and need give no reason for his refusal. If a customer is refused drink in the Public Bar, however, he can bring the matter up at the next sessions of the Licensing Bench.

Note: the licensing laws are responsible for so many anomalies that London drinkers are apt to consider them particularly unreasonable. Experience of other countries tends, however, to make one feel that licensing laws are unreasonable wherever they are in force. Personally I have been surprised to find I could not order brandy in Brussels or whisky in a train passing through Texas; and nothing in London is quite so comic as the regulation in Washington, D.C., by which you have to sit on a stool to drink beer and at a table to drink whisky. Nor have we any sight to show so pathetic as the queues at the Government liquor stores in Montreal on a Saturday night, or so prim as Canada's system of men's and women's beverage parlours.

LIGHT ALE. A very light bottled beer, usually highly aerated.

LONG PULL. An old custom of giving the customer extra value by serving rather more than he ordered and paid for, killed by the ban on treating during the 1914-1918 war and never revived. Under existing laws the landlord can be fined for giving either a Long Pull or a Short Pull. A survival of the Long Pull is nevertheless to be found in the custom by which some pubs, if you start with pints and then go on to halves in the same tankards, guess the measure and give you a good deal more than halves.

LOUNGE. A superior sort of bar, usually with tables, often with service, sometimes without draught beer. (See *Saloon Lounge*, and pp. 30-33.)

LUNCH-BAR. A bar with a refreshment counter offering cold snacks and sometimes hot meals too. Saloon prices are always charged in the Lunch-Bar.

MILD ALE. The lightest and cheapest draught beer, the staple drink in Public Bars, where 'a pint' without qualification means a pint of mild. Much drunk by darts-players. Also mixed with bitter, Burton, stout, or strong ale. (See also *Ale*.)

MOTHER-IN-LAW. A facetious name for stout-and-bitter.

MOTHER'S RUIN. Similarly, a name for gin, especially with hot water.

NIP. A name for any small quantity of spirits or wine; a single whisky; an odd-sized measure less than half-a-pint, used for strong ales and barley wines, draught or bottled. (See also *Pony*.)

NUMBER I. A name given by some breweries to their *strong ale* (q.v.) both bottled and draught. 'Bass No. 1' is probably the best-known barley wine. It is very good for cold weather but it is expensive compared with other beers and of very high gravity, and it is not seen much since the war.

OFF-LICENCE. This is an important rival to the jug-and-bottle bar. Many grocers and wine-merchants have an off-licence, but 'the off-licence' usually means a special shop kept for the sale of beer for consumption off the premises, where draught as well as bottled beer can be obtained. These are sometimes run in conjunction with a pub, but when last the figures were published, there were 2,000 separate off-licences in the County of London.

Note: the popular opinion of the off-licence, as compared with the genuine pub, is perfectly illustrated by the comedians' joke: 'Where did you get married—in church?' 'No—we went to one of those off-licence places.'

OLD, in London pubs, means *Burton* (q.v.). These variants are used quite arbitrarily. For instance, Burton (or old) mixed with mild ale is usually asked for as old-and-mild, not mild-and-Burton or old-and-ale, but if you want to mix Burton with bitter you ask for bitter-and-Burton (or B-B), not for old-and-bitter. Euphony probably has a lot to do with this. 'Old-and-ale', for instance, which I have only once heard, is a hard phrase to say and very searching on the vowel sounds.

OPTIC or OPTICAL. The trade name for an automatic measuring tap for serving spirits, used in many pubs. The bottle is fixed upside-down and the 'optic' is a glass disc fastened to its neck from which an exact tot of liquor is discharged when the tap is turned. This is designed to prevent a bad barman or barmaid giving short measure, but if you once get a bad barman or barmaid, no mechanical device can do that.

PALE ALE usually stands for bottled beer: a clear yellow drink with plenty of froth, often containing a good deal of gas. Speaking very roughly pale ale among bottled beers corresponds to bitter among draught beers, as brown ale does to Burton, but some breweries do a bottled bitter and some do a draught pale ale.

PEWTER is probably the best material for doing justice to the taste of draught beer and it was once commonly used for drinking vessels in the pubs, but in London it has now been largely displaced by *glass* (q.v.). Pewter is mostly confined to the Saloon Bar and very often to the regulars there, and it is the modern alloy, which is harder and shinier than the old. Behind the bar the term is sometimes used for the washing-up sink.

Note: one of the few houses that tried to replace its old pewter (which was frequently stolen) with good modern pewter, not too like Britannia metal, was the Cheshire Cheese off Fleet Street. The new stuff was however stolen with such rapidity that they took to serving their beer in earthenware mugs. A classic of the old pewter-pinching days is the Phil May joke about the landlord examining a half-crown offered by a really seedy customer. 'I don't so much mind your pinching my pewters', he says, 'but when it comes to bringing 'em back in the shape of 'arf crowns it's a bit too much'.

PIG'S EAR. Rhyming slang for beer.

PIN-TABLES are now firmly established in the pubs; they have largely driven out old-fashioned games like table skittles, and the second generation of pin-tables with bells ringing, lights flashing, and automatic scoring has long ago driven out the original game based on Corinthian bagatelle. The pin-tables give the customer an excuse to stay on after he has had his lunch or the drink he came in for, and of course they are even more profitable if customers play each other for drinks. There are strict laws against any kind of gaming in pubs, so if the landlord does give a drink or a packet of cigarettes for an outstanding score it has to be done on the sly; but not many landlords are giving away either drinks or cigarettes now.

PINT. Pints were once the ordinary measure for draught beer but before the war they were becoming rare in the Saloon Bar; in fact some houses were so refined as not to keep pint pots or glasses on that side. The weakening of beer has brought the pint into favour again even in the Saloon, and in the Public Bar it has always been the standard order.

Note: the Imperial pint is one-eighth of a gallon, half of a quart, four times a gill, or 20 ounces. It is in this last respect that Imperial pints, quarts, and gallons differ from American. The U.S. ounce is larger than the Imperial ounce (1 U.S. oz. = 29.57 c.c. and 1 Imperial oz. = 28.41 c.c., so 1 U.S. oz. = 1.04 Imperial oz.), but the U.S. pint holds only 16 U.S. oz. against the 20 oz. in an Imperial pint, and the U.S. pint is therefore less than ours by nearly 6 cubic inches. This difference becomes more important, naturally, as you go up the scale; the American 'quart' is not nearly so big as our quart and the American gallon, at 128 U.S. ounces, is .833 of an Imperial gallon at 160 oz. The net result of all this is that once you get past Bermuda you never get what a London pub-goer would recognise as a pint of beer, even if he succeeds in finding anything bigger than a 12-ounce glass in an American bar.

Note 2: the measures used in the pub business are complicated by the fact that the bottle of spirits holds a pint and a third. This is the 'reported quart,' which is two-thirds of the Imperial quart. Spirit measures are made in fractions of a pint but are usually referred to as fractions of a quartern (or gill): 'four out,' 'five out', etc., mean four or five to a quartern. Counting in this fashion you soon get into fractions, e.g. a measure of $\frac{1}{14}$ of a pint gives $3\frac{1}{2}$ out of the gill and $18\frac{2}{3}$ tots to the bottle. The only spirits measure that the London pub-goer need bother much about is however the standard $\frac{1}{24}$ of a pint, which gives 6 out of the quartern and 32 singles to the bottle. That is all he is likely to get.

Ounces are used in trade catalogues for wine and liqueur glasses but I have never seen them specified on a price-list in London as I have, for instance, on American trains. At the 'six out' measure a single whisky works out at .83 of an Imperial ounce and a double at 1.6, so perhaps this is just as well.

PONY. A measure smaller than a half-pint (usually a gill), used mostly for a last drink taken as a gesture of goodwill when the drinker does not really want any more.

PORT, taken with or without lemon, is surprisingly popular in the pubs. Both men and women drink it, the latter often under the influence of the old belief that it does not rank as an alcoholic drink.

PORTER is obsolete in the London pubs, though its name survives on the beer-pulls of some unmodernised houses, and the name is used in some off-licences. It was originally to stout as X is to XX, and in that sense it is still widely popular in Ireland.

POT. Formerly, a name for a tankard, usually a quart. Not now used in the pubs, but a pot still means a quart in the off-licence trade.

PRIVATE BAR. A compartment half-way between the Public Bar and the Saloon Bar, now tending to disappear. Where it is found it is rather apt to deputise for the *Ladies' Bar* (q.v.).

PUBLIC BAR. The plebeian side of the pub, where everything is cheapest, where nothing is charged for decoration, where pints of ale are the most popular drink, where there are no pin-tables, and darts, shove-ha'penny, and dominoes are played by people who have played them all their lives. (See pp. 38-41.)

PUBLIC-HOUSE. Throughout this book the terms 'public-house' and 'pub' have been used loosely for places where they sell alcoholic drinks on draught and in bottle for consumption on the premises. This is the sense in which they are used by the ordinary man. Technically, however, there is a distinction between public-houses, which are licensed to sell all kinds of drinks, and beer-houses, which are not licensed for spirits. There are also licences for wine, sweets, and cider, and off-licences, issued by the Licensing Justices. Theatres and clubs are not licensed by the Justices.

Note: one of the difficulties in writing this book has been to decide what is and what is not a pub in the ordinary sense of the word. All bars are not pubs, but it is hard to draw a dividing line. For instance, I have mentioned Regent Street as a street without a pub of its own, because Verrey's, although it sells draught beer, appears to me a restaurant with a bar rather than a pub. On the other hand I count the Rose of Normandy as a pub rather than a restaurant, and in the evening it certainly is. I have tried to find a logical basis for distinction but I am afraid I have had to fall back on taste and fancy again.

QUART. A quarter of a gallon, or two pints. Quart measures were once common in London pubs but it is years since they have been generally used, though many houses have quart tankards for display purposes which can be taken down and dusted if they are really required. Quart bottles used to be largely favoured for taking home, in the days when you could take beer home, and they are still often used in pubs for serving bottled drinks; a customer who orders a light or a brown seldom complains if his drink is poured out of a quart bottle instead of his getting a half-pint bottle to himself.

QUARTERN. A measure for spirits, not now used when ordering them in a pub. Before the 1914 war a large Scotch was a quartern and a small Scotch a half-quartern. Wartime Restrictions brought in the 'Lloyd George measure', which worked out at six 'drops' to the quartern, or 'six out' of the gill (q.v.), and the single has never advanced beyond this again. Comparison of these quantities, remembering also the comparative prices, helps one to realise how much more serious an affair drinking must have been before 1914.

RED BIDDY. A drink made of cheap red wine fortified with spirits, which became popular in the thirties. For its price it was extremely intoxicating, and it had the quality (like bad potheen) of making its addicts fight. The nature of the drink is well indicated by its nick-name—Lunatic's Broth. It was a real scourge in Glasgow, but it never got the same hold in London.

RINGS. A game played by throwing rings at hooks in a board hung on the wall, which was once played extensively in the London pubs but has now quite gone out.

ROUGH. Strictly speaking, the beer in the drip-cans, made up of residue from the bottoms of bottles and overflows from glasses of draught, which is not normally sold in London pubs. Colloquially used for the cheapest beer (i.e. ordinary mild ale), and with a more clearly facetious bearing for other drinks. If you ask for a can of rough in a West-End bar where they sell only bitter you will get bitter; but before asking for it in an ordinary pub it is as well to be sure the landlord knows what you mean. This use of the word has no connection with Rough Cider, which is sold in cider-houses but in few other London pubs.

RUM is perhaps the least popular spirituous drink in the London pubs; before the war it was largely drunk by taxi-drivers, and with hot water by people who had colds, but it never competed in favour with whisky or gin. The vagaries of export have made it a most ubiquitous drink nowadays; some pubs even have a printed notice saying: VERY LITTLE WHISKY, SOME GIN, PLENTY OF RUM.

SALOON BAR. The superior bar in an ordinary London pub. (See p. 34.)

SALOON LOUNGE. A refinement on the Saloon Bar. (See p. 30.)

SCOTCH. The usual abbreviation for Scotch whisky, the most popular spirituous drink in the London pubs. The half-dozen or so most-advertised brands are to be seen (at intervals) in every house with a spirits licence.

SCOTCH ALE. A brown beer rather resembling Burton. In the London pubs the term almost invariably stands for Younger's Scotch Ale, in bottle or on draught, which is a genuine Scottish brew. As this is a very popular drink it is often to be found in free houses, where it usually replaces a Burton, though there are pubs that sell both. Younger's Scotch Ale is their No. 3. Their No. 1 is a really strong brew.

SCOTCH HOUSE, or SCOTS HOOSE, is a name anybody can use, but in London it is likely to mean a Younger house, where you may find a lot of tartans and a slightly olde-worlde air, but you will certainly find their Scotch Ale on draught.

SHADES. Originally a generic term for cellars, now the name of one famous pub at Charing Cross and of various London bars. When used for one bar in an ordinary pub, roughly equivalent to *Dive*.

SHANDY, or SHANDY-GAFF. A drink composed of beer mixed with ginger-beer or lemonade (lemon shandy), popular in hot weather and drunk at other times by people who do not want to drink too much beer. Also drunk nowadays by people who would rather have beer, during the hot weather when beer is in short supply and the landlord refuses to serve it straight. Made half-and-half it is a good summer drink, but in these conditions they may give you two small bottles of lemonade before filling up the pint with beer, thus making what used to be known as lemon-with-a-dash, which is practically a soft drink.

SHERRY is drunk in pubs more extensively than any other wine except port, but it varies in quality.

SHOVE-HA'PENNY has been played in the pubs from time immemorial, and it is a very skilled game. It has one advantage over darts in that it can be played in a very small space—wherever there is room for a table, in fact, as hardened players do not seem to mind being jostled from behind.

SINGLE. A small measure of whisky, gin, or rum, as opposed to *Double*. A pub single is the smallest amount of drink yet known to man.

SNACK BAR. A bar specialising in food, particularly cold food— sandwiches, cold cooked meats, crab, lobster, etc. Saloon prices are charged for drinks in the Snack Bar.

SNORT. An American term for a shot, nip, or drop (whisky usually understood). The term invaded London pubs only during the war, when the Short Snorter club was formed. The idea was that if you had flown the Atlantic or been flown across it you gave somebody else who had flown it two dollar bills, one for himself and one on which he endorsed your exploit and constituted you a Short Snorter. So far as I remember you were supposed to be able to claim a drink or a dollar from any other Short Snorter you met in a pub who could not produce his testimonial bill, as with the old 'Froth-Blowers' club, but except in bars much frequented by Americans, such as the Bolivar near Broadcasting House, this never happened to me. Some people however entered into the spirit of the thing and acquired long strings of dollars, pounds, francs, lire, occupation marks, and all sorts of other currencies, stuck together and garnished with the autographs of the thousands of people who flew the Atlantic during the war.

SNUG. An Irish term for a semi-private compartment in a pub; the nearest London equivalent is a bar parlour, or the sort of inner sanctum you find in the Devereux or the Goat.

SODA-WATER is drunk extensively in Saloon Bars, etc., with all kinds of spirits—whisky, gin, and brandy, and even rum. In hot weather it is occasionally drunk with beer; either beer with a dash of soda or, more often, soda with a dash of beer.

SPLASH. A tot of soda-water from the siphon, usually given free with spirits; as opposed to the bottled brands.

STOUT in bottle is served in all London pubs. The most widely drunk stout is Guinness, but most breweries have their own brands and sell them in their own houses, often at prices considerably below that of Guinness. Draught stout is less common than it used to be, as it requires careful keeping and a fairly quick sale. In Watney houses, for instance, where Reid's stout in bottle costs little more than draught beer, it is not much use asking for draught stout. The introduction of the metal container for Guinness has however given a new fillip to the habit of drinking stout on draught. (See pp. 17 and 18.) Stout is of course largely drunk with oysters, and it can also be mixed with champagne to form *Black Velvet* (q.v.), but both these habits really belong to a more lavish age.

Note: stout has a considerable export market, as I discovered on my first visit abroad, when a waiter at the Gare de Lyon, spotting my pronunciation of 'bière', asked me whether I wanted *pell-ell ou stoot*. It is surprisingly appropriate in hot climates; I believe it is stocked on ships going to India, and I found a bar in Havana where the proprietors, one of whom was English by origin, kept baby Guinness for their own consumption and were not over-pleased when I cut in on their supplies. Besides Guinness, Bass's stout, which is made for export only, and Barclay's Russian stout have a great reputation abroad. I had a remarkable experience with Bass's stout in a casino in Normandy, when the barman divulged that he had half-a-dozen bottles that had been there when he took over three seasons before, and had not served them because he did not know how long stout would keep. I said that properly bottled it would keep for ever, so we had them up and drank them between us; they were very hard to pour but when you got a glass-full it was nectar. Our reaction was so conspicuous that the other customers began ordering stout too, but they got the current vintage and could not make out what our transports were about.

STRONG ALE or STRONG BEER. Sometimes 'strong ale' is merely a pseudonym for the ordinary Burton, which is not particularly strong. But nearly every brewery has a good strong ale, and although war and post-war conditions militate against strong beers, if you see a little barrel on the counter marked with an unusual number of X's (or K's) and find that it costs a good deal more than the ordinary draught beer, it is usually worth trying. Most houses where they keep strong ale on draught keep it only in the winter. Famous strong ales are Bass No. 1, Younger's No. 1, and Benskin's Colne Spring. The last, which is a bottled beer, is the joy of connoisseurs. Benskin's licensees are not supposed to serve more than four bottles of Colne Spring to any one customer—and four bottles is quite enough. (See *Barley Wine, Number 1.*).

SUDS. A facetious term for beer, based on the soapy appearance of the froth; as in 'a bucket of suds'.

SWIPES. Waste beer; used colloquially for ale, etc., like *Rough* (q.v.),

TANKARD. A drinking vessel with a handle, as opposed to an ordinary glass. Pewter is the traditional material but it is becoming rare in London pubs, where the ordinary tankard is now made of glass, though earthenware is sometimes used. There is no connection between size and shape; you are as likely to get a pint in a straight glass as a half in a mug. (See *Can, Glass, Pewter, Pot.*).

TAP, or TAP-ROOM. Originally used for the plebian bar in a hotel yard, or for the brewery's own serving-bar (Brewery Tap); now not often encountered in London, though one of my own locals—the Phoenix in Palace Street, which backs on to Watney's Pimlico Brewery—uses the name for a room opening out of the Public Bar where people take their lunch.

TEETOTAL drinks are supplied in all pubs, though naturally the bigger houses have a more extensive range. Soda and tonic water are sold wherever spirits are sold, and most houses catering for mixed custom sell things like lime juice and orangeade. You cannot count, however, upon walking into a pub and obtaining a cup of tea on demand.

TIED HOUSE. A pub in which one brewery has the monopoly of supplying the beer. Most London pubs are now tied. (See *Free House.*)

TONIC WATER is drunk extensively in the pubs, mostly (though not entirely) with gin.

'THE TRADE' is an expression used in political and sociological discussions to represent the whole of the interests benefiting financially by the sale of drink.

Note: as there is so much politics about anything to do with drinking, it might be as well to state explicitly that this book has been neither inspired nor encouraged—much less subsidised—by the Trade.

WALLOP. A name for mild ale, particularly used by darts-players.

WHISKEY and WHISKY. Correctly, whiskey is Irish and whisky is Scotch. The latter is very much more popular in London pubs, where whisky and Scotch are almost interchangeable terms. Irish whiskey is not much drunk outside the Irish houses, except when there is no Scotch. The dollar shortage has caused transatlantic whisky to disappear, though Canadian Club used to be fairly well known in the West End before the war. This was a rye; I cannot remember ever seeing a Bourbon in a London pub. (See *Irish, Scotch.*) *Note:* the Scottish custom of putting whisky in beer is almost unknown in London. I once had to interpret, in Mooney's in the Strand, between a K.O.S.B. man who wanted to order two pints of beer with whiskies in them and the Dublin boy behind the bar, who had never heard of such a thing.

WINE can usually be obtained in London pubs, and there have been times in the last few years when it was all you could get, but it is not always wise to drink it in pubs you don't know, if you can possibly get anything else.

WINE BAR. Some pubs have a bar called by this name where they specialise in wines and spirits, usually selling bottled beer but not draught beer. The price factor makes the Wine Bar even more select than the Saloon.

WINE HOUSE or WINE LODGE. A sub-species of pub specialising in wines, and usually giving better value than the ordinary pub both in quality and in bulk. Wine houses are apt to have no draught beer. (See pp. 54-57.)

WINTER ALE. A name for a strong ale; a more precise term is October Ale.

WOMPO. A name for the best ale, used in the East End and around the docks.

WOOD. Beer from the wood is beer drawn directly from the cask, with an ordinary tap, as opposed to beer pumped up by means of a beer-engine. Many connoisseurs think that this vastly improves the flavour of the beer. Wine can often be obtained from the wood, and spirits sometimes, the distinction here being that it is drawn direct from the cask without having been bottled.

WORKMAN'S DINNER. A pre-war institution was the meal served under this name in many Public Bars, consisting mainly of a cut from the joint and two veg. and costing a shilling or less.

INDEX
OF PUBS MENTIONED

This is not meant to be a list of the best pubs in London, or Where to Go for a Drink. It is merely a list of the pubs mentioned in this book, and as each of them was mentioned to illustrate some particular point the selection has its vagaries. Some of my own favourite pubs are not in the list, and some that are by no means my favourites are. Some are not even open now, so it would be most unwise to treat this Index as a guide without first referring to the text.

The street names are included for identification, as so many pubs often share the same name. I hope they are all up to date, but it is very difficult to keep pace with the L.C.C.